"*Chris has an extraordinary gift – one that psychologist Lewis Smedes refers to as 'magic eyes' – the gift to look at the ordinary things in our lives through the eyes of grace. Read this book and do it soon--- it will re-awaken your heart and restore magic to your eyes.*"

Chris Ellerman, CEO, Outreach Community Ministries

"*Chris's writing is filled with warmth and insight. This book made me glad to be alive and eager to find glimpses of grace in my own life.*"

Kevin Miller
Author of <u>Surviving Information Overload</u>

"*The real life stories in <u>Glimpsing Grace in Ordinary Days</u> remind us to slow down and open our eyes to the spiritual realities of God's grace at work in the common and everyday occurrences of life.*"

Diane Jordan, Director, Children's Ministries at College Church, Wheaton, IL.

Glimpsing Grace in Ordinary Days

Christine Litavsky

CROSSLINK
PUBLISHING

Glimpsing Grace in Ordinary Days

Ɗ CrossLink Publishing
Ȼ www.crosslinkpublishing.com

ISBN 978-1-936746-60-6
Library of Congress Control Number: 2013940234

Cover art by Janice Zeuch.

Acknowledgements

Thank you Kristen Shikany, my true friend and valued editor! I couldn't have done this without you.

And thanks to Jim Bowen, who never, ever stopped asking me when I was going to publish this book. You always had confidence in me.

Dedication

To my greatest encourager, my husband Keith.

Table of Contents

Preface

I 'll never forget my first college writing class. My professor paced back and forth in front of us with his hands clasped behind his back. He stopped, faced us, and declared: "Effective writers write about what they know." That statement, along with hefty required doses of E.B. White, helped me understand the power of authentic, honest writing.

That's why, when I landed a weekly newspaper column many years later, I wrote about my life – ordinary events in the life of an ordinary woman. After all, that's what I knew! This chronicling had an unexpected benefit: to find column material I was forced to slow down and really mull through my days. I'd turn an event over and over in my mind, pushing and pulling at it, taking it apart and piecing it back together. Usually, even a common occurrence would take on new meaning once I pondered it a bit. Perhaps for the first time, I understood the opening line of Henry David Thoreau's *Walden*: "I went to the woods because I wished to live deliberately." I wasn't living in the woods, but I was striving to become more deliberate in my examination of ordinary events.

As my columns accumulated, I realized many had a common thread, one that readers were recognizing and embracing: They focused on the grace notes that we often forget to listen to during our frenzied days.

Since my column ended, I've had hundreds of folks of various stripes ask me to publish a collection of my columns as a book. It's from these requests that *Glimpsing Grace in Ordinary Days* was born. About half of this book is comprised of previously published columns – my favorites and judging by email responses, my reader's favorites as well. They've been slightly expanded, as I'm no longer constrained by word count (hurrah!) or secular constrictions (it's incredibly freeing to write for a Christian publisher!). The other half is comprised of material new to this book.

Glimpsing Grace in Ordinary Days is a book about finding grace in all areas of daily life. It helps readers pull often-elusive glimmers of grace out of our chaotic world, examine them, and rest in the assurance that God is always at work.

Some days grace abounds; it's impossible to miss. These are the good days, and plenty of them are showcased in this book. There are other days that seem so ordinary we don't recognize the grace shining within them. I write about these too.

Some days, however, aren't as beautiful. At times, we are overwhelmed with the realities of a fallen world and become immune to the grace notes playing around us. These are the hard days, and they are also part of this book. They can become easier – or at least a bit more redeemable – when grace is recognized.

While we live our ordinary lives with their highs and lows, we need to remember that glimpsing grace often must be deliberate. We must receive a gift before we can open and enjoy it, and that's what grace is: a gift from God that is undeserved and given because He loves us.

This gift can take many forms. It can be a stepparent, a lake, or a baby turtle. It can be an Easter egg hunt, a memory, or simply a second chance to make things right. Perhaps Frederick Buechner said it best: "Grace is something you can never get but can only be given. There's no way to earn it or deserve it or bring it about any more than you can deserve the taste of raspberries and cream or earn good looks. A good night's sleep is grace and so are good dreams. Most tears are grace. The smell of rain is grace. Somebody loving you is grace."

My prayer is that *Glimpsing Grace in Ordinary Days* helps you remember to slow down and ruminate on the glimpses of grace in *your* life. There are many. We just need to look for them.

Thoreau also wrote that "{he} wanted to live deep and suck out the marrow of life." He called it marrow; I call it grace. Whatever you call it, it's rich and satisfying. Enjoy it.

Chapter 1: The Meaning Of Family

"There is no such thing as a "broken family." Family is family, and is not determined by marriage certificates, divorce papers, and adoption documents. Families are made in the heart."

—C. JoyBell C.

Les

T here's so much comfort in the truth of the biblical statement: *"And we know that in all things God works for the good of those who love him, who have been called according to his purpose"* (Rom 8:28). Unfortunately, this verse is often misunderstood. It does not mean (alas!) that only good things will happen to those who love God. But it does mean God can make some pretty great things spring from life's more sour moments. And for many of us, sour moments are far too common. It can, therefore, be a great comfort to believe that our greatest blessings may actually come out of our misfortunes.

I've been pondering this verse because one of the biggest blessings of my life has recently left this earth. This blessing, my stepfather, was provided to me and my family because of a terrible misfortune that occurred in my life. When I was eight years old, my parents got divorced.

As divorces go, it was relatively amicable. But it was still traumatic for my brother and me. I remember what cartoon I was watching the Saturday morning my parents called me downstairs to tell me the news. I remember where I was sitting. I remember the questions I asked. I don't remember anything else in my first eight years as clearly as that morning. I know, from talking to people who have suffered great loss or trauma, that my crystal clear memory of the event is not unusual. It's as if great shock somehow imprints itself into our memories whether we want it to or not. And a shock it was. I had never heard of divorce; I didn't even know it existed. No one I knew had divorced parents; no one had a dad living in a separate house. I remember thinking, in a moment of mature clarity, that I would from that point on be forever different than my friends and neighbors. Nothing would ever be the same.

I was right. Nothing was ever the same after that, but something wonderful eventually did occur from that surreal morning. Seven years later, my mother married a wonderful man, my stepfather Les. And wasn't it a coincidence that he lived right next door to us? My mother had lost a husband to divorce; Les had lost his wife to cancer. Both were grieving. Both were struggling. Both had a lot of love to give.

They decided to give it to each other and their combined children. After dating for several years, they got married, sold one house and settled in the other. They were married for almost twenty-five years.

The ultimate gift Les gave to our family was love. He was brimming with it; he loved people without reserve. He was never afraid to say the words "I love you" or just show it by a calm acceptance of people from all walks of life. My friends, and especially my brother's friends, sensed this. Our house was a place where they always felt welcome, either for dinner or an extra bed. No judgments were made; instead compassion and steadiness abounded to calm even the most distraught teenager.

Part of this was due to the simple fact that Les had practical experience with teenage angst; he had already raised three children. Twenty years older than my mother, he had an understanding of what was truly important and was a pillar of calmness in our teenage years. You see, Les had not only lost his wife to cancer, but he had lost his daughter to cancer as well. She was only in her twenties. I cannot imagine what he went through during those years; all I know is by the time he was dealing with my teenage sulks or my brother's more wild antics, he was firm when needed, genuinely compassionate, and able to put things in proper perspective.

Not only did Les teach me a lot about calmness and loving, but he also gave me an extended family that I cannot imagine my life without. His two sons and their families are true family to me— I was at their weddings, present as a godmother at baptisms, and have shared in their joys and sorrows throughout the years. His sister, who is also now gone, was a calming force in my life when I had three little ones and no attention span. She would bring over coffee cake and spend hours teaching me to crochet. His nephew and his girlfriend have been life rafts to my mother now that Les is gone, and are never happier than when we're all gathered around a table. Like families everywhere, we've had our share of squabbles, but we are, through Les, forever woven together in this life. I am so grateful for that.

Some of my life's greatest blessings—my stepfather and his family—would have never come about if not for that horrible event that happened in 1976. I have not changed my opinion that the divorce of my parents was traumatic. I have not forgotten some of its effects on me and my brother. The first few years were especially rough. As the only children in the neighborhood with divorced parents, we were excluded from birthday parties and other invitations. One memory that particularly stings is finding my brother in tears because he couldn't join Cub Scouts. You see, to join your mother had to volunteer to run one pack meeting during the year, and my mother had to go back to work after the divorce. She simply could not leave a job to run a mid-afternoon Cub Scouts meeting, and no exceptions were made; my brother could not participate. It was a rotten time.

But from that time came years of joy. An extended, larger family. Another loving Grandpa for my children. And a source of continual calmness, love and acceptance.

I will miss Les more than I can say. But I am thanking God for His goodness in bringing him into our lives. He not only selflessly helped raise two more teenagers, but he illustrated an important theological truth for me in a way I could understand it. God will make goodness evolve from this fallen world. Despite the mess we often make of our lives, we are treated with grace. And grace is what Les truly was for me.

Grandparents and Graduations

As high school graduations roll around once again, I'm realizing something startling. I can't really remember my own graduation at all. I cannot tell you which student we chose to give the commencement speech. I have no recollection of anyone else speaking. I don't remember what my gown looked like, I don't remember switching the tassel on my cap, I don't remember throwing my cap into the air. I only remember a vast feeling of relief. I liked high school—at times quite a lot—but senior year I found myself chomping at the bit. I was tired of hall passes, gym class, rumors and cliques. Graduation seemed like liberation. I never wanted to look back.

For over twenty years I didn't. I had too many other things to think about; high school seemed like an abstract idea. Lately, however, I've been invited to graduation parties for the children of my friends, unbelievable in and of itself. As I watch these delighted 18 year olds revel in ceremonies and parties, I've been renewing my efforts to remember my own graduation. To that end, I finally unearthed some graduation pictures, and when I fanned them out and really studied them I became a bit disquieted. I realized I was so self-absorbed at my graduation I didn't appreciate the people who surrounded me that day.

People like my grandparents, who traveled many miles to join in my success. People like my divorced parents, who set aside old hurts and grudges to come together and make my day a joy. At the time I thought nothing of that effort; now I realize my parents always worked together to make family events as normal as possible. I never really appreciated it until now.

One picture stands out from the rest. I'm sitting in front of my graduation cake flanked by two sets of beaming grandparents. One set was my mother's parents; the other was my stepmother's parents. My throat constricted when I looked at the proud faces of my step-grandparents who loved me unconditionally and weren't afraid to show it. My admiration grew for my maternal grandparents who were always my stalwarts and never threatened by the appearance of new grandparents. In the middle of the adoring throng, I sat sporting my newly minted class of 1985 tee shirt. I look tan, rested, and impossibly young.

What pains me about this photo is I don't remember it being taken. In fact, I have only the dimmest recollection of the family party given in my honor. Both sets of grandparents had traveled cross-country for the occasion. My step-parents and parents worked together on party details, including gifts. Neighbors and friends were there as well, yet the party itself is very dim to me.

This is because I wasn't conscious of the party even as it was happening around me. Instead, during the festivities, I was planning my evening agenda. I was fretting over which party to attend, and with whom. I was strategizing an extension of my curfew, and hopping up repeatedly to answer phone calls. I was mentally planning an outfit for the evening that included my stepsister's sweater. Would she let me borrow it? How soon could I gracefully bow out of the family obligations and begin the evening? When would everyone release me to do what I really wanted to do, which was to celebrate with my fellow classmates, not my grandparents and parents?

The irony of this self-centeredness is that most—not all, but most—of the fellow 18-year-olds I was so excited to see on graduation night are no longer a part of my life. They were important to me for only a period, and then they faded away. Yet because of my youth, I wanted to be with them more than my own family. In fact, I wanted to be with them so much I was mentally checked out of the family party in my honor.

I would love to have that day back with my grandparents, who are all gone now. I miss them and would feel privileged to treasure their company and revel in their pride. But, as we all know, we cannot go back. We need to keep that in mind while we go about our daily walk. We need to remember the people in our lives who are truly important, and try—and sometimes it's very hard – to always appreciate them, and tell them so. They are gifts to us from God.

I mentioned finding the graduation pictures to my mother and stepfather, stressing how blessed I felt that, despite having divorced parents, I never had to worry about parents and stepfamilies getting along and working together. Major events were firmly celebrated in a central location by all sides of the family. I confessed guilt that I didn't appreciate that enough.

They looked a bit startled. "That's how it should be for any child," they insisted. "It was our job, as the adults, to allow you to be a rather typical teenager." They waved away further credit.

I pondered that and felt a bit better about things. After all, if there had been tension, or fighting, or traveling back and forth to different houses, or fights between the step and biological grandparents, I might indeed have distinct memories of the day. And they would not be pleasant. My good, if hazy, recollections have gained some merit in my mind. Instead of being ashamed of their vagueness, I'm learning to be grateful for them. I'm grateful for the security that surrounded me which enabled me to be self-absorbed.

And most of all, I'm grateful I'm no longer in high school.

Newport Summers

M any of us have a place. A place we return to time and again. A place that calms us and makes everything seem right. Our places can be anywhere and any size, but they all have one thing in common: we would rather be there than anywhere in the world, and memories of it can lull us to sleep during a bad night.

For me, that place is Lake Memphremagog in Newport, Vermont. My grandparents spent every summer there since their 1932 honeymoon, renting different cottages each year. In 1966 they bought a cottage of their own, and the family has gathered there ever since. Until I was 18, I spent a good chunk of every summer there. After that, working for college expenses took priority, and my visits there became shorter, yet somehow sweeter.

Northern Vermont is beautiful, with pastoral farm scenes and rolling hills. The lake our cottage hugs is huge, spring-fed, and full of creatures. The air is absolutely crisp and fragrant with clover, and the night sky is clear and twinkling with stars. When you drift off to sleep, the only sound you hear is the water gently lapping against the rocks.

I think of Vermont whenever I feel stressed and unmoored. Because to me, Vermont is more than a place. It's security. It's always been there, solid and unchanging in my ever-changing life. Whenever I return, it's as though I've never left. And every time I leave, I weep.

My grandparent's cottage transports me back to the early seventies. The sheets and towels neatly folded and labeled in the linen closet are the same ones I used as a small child. The furniture and braided rugs were placed there more than 40 years ago and still remain. The window treatments, lovingly made by my grandma, hang exactly the way she hung them decades earlier. The worn Willow Ware china sits in the corner hutch in the dining room. The coffee mugs still hang on the pegged holder my grandfather crafted. It's fascinating to me that my father's name still graces his hook on this cup hanger – my parents have been divorced for over 30 years.

Time has somehow passed by this place.

And of course, the lake itself is still the same, as are the massive granite blocks that shore up our property from the water. These blocks are each unique in color, shape and size, and can never be moved by man alone. Some are flat, some are rough-hewn, and all have flecks in them that glisten in the sunlight and moonlight. As a child, I had my favorites. They are still there, waiting for me every visit. The granite countertop craze makes me smile; I've thought granite was beautiful since I could toddle and never thought it had any other purpose than keeping water away from a house.

The lake has an earthy smell and taste that cannot be replicated, and I've tasted more than my share of it. Clear, clean and very cold, it's where I learned to swim, waterski and fish. We did a lot of fishing. We caught bass, bluegill, perch and occasionally, a pickerel. If they were large enough, and many were, my grandfather would clean them as my brother and I watched in delighted horror. To this day I can remember all the steps of the process, one I've never embarked upon myself. After watching the cleaning, my appetite was shot and I never enjoyed eating the fish. I always begged, and received, a hot dog during our fish lunches instead.

Vermont was where I truly understood God was a creator God. The aquatic life He spoke into being was varied and fascinating. My brother and I collected loads of crayfish, frogs, snails, crabs, water bugs and clams. We made an aquarium in our Radio Flyer wagon so we could examine our creatures closely. My grandfather, ever the conservationist, closely monitored our progress and ensured anything we caught was safely returned to the water.

The water creature that trumped all others was one we never caught, and never ventured near. It was The Snapping Turtle.

The Snapping Turtle always came into our boathouse to lay her eggs. She was absolutely fearsome looking; mud-colored with a pointy-looking shell and a sharp beak. She was quite large, probably the size of a small bike tire. We were fascinated with her and terrified of her at the same time.

Whether or not it was the same turtle every year can be debated; there were probably dozens of them in that lake, but my brother and I were convinced the same turtle returned every year to our boathouse to terrorize us and whenever we spotted her I would not go into the water for several hours. Even if my grandpa offered waterskiing, I held firm. With my luck, I'd fall while skiing and land on top of the startled turtle, and she would have no other recourse than to attack. My grandfather must have really grappled with his store of patience at my fear, but aside from a slight lifting of the eyebrows, he never said much. I would watch in horrified admiration as he jumped in the lake to swim even when the turtle was still in sight. That he was never attacked failed to move me; he was just lucky.

On land we saw entire families of spotted skunks waddling in lines, and calmly conversed in the twilight with bats flittering around our heads catching bugs. We saw sleek minks weaving in and out of the granite blocks, and a red fox sunning itself on the boathouse veranda. My brother and I were students of nature during those Newport Summers, but most importantly, we learned about family.

We were schooled in the art of family tradition. We were taught how wonderful it was to eat breakfast together every morning, without any background noise except the waves. No matter what was going on during the day, we broke for lunch and sat together at the picnic table passing around platters of cold cuts, baskets of different breads, and pitchers of iced tea so cold it hurt our teeth. I remember squirming with boredom as my grandpa methodically peeled an apple with his pocketknife and my grandmother took a half an hour to eat an open-faced sandwich, but we were expected to sit politely and wait, and we did. When everyone was done, my brother and I were excused to do the dishes, which we did as quickly as possible so we could jump back into the water. We were shown the grace of gathering at twilight with drinks and munchies to look over the calm lake and rehash the day. We reveled in playing games together after dinner, talking and laughing till bedtime. We learned every variation of poker and played for pennies that were kept safely in labeled containers for the next summer. My penny container is still the same Blue Bonnet Margarine tub I secured when I was six.

Vermont was about being together.

That's why every summer I'm not there, I miss it. But I know even if I were to never get there again (and that's not the plan) I would still have my memories. Memories of talking, fishing, playing cards, eating lobster and petting calves at the barn down the street. Memories of spending time together visiting and enjoying simple things. Just envisioning the taste of the water and the smell of the meadows helps me relax—no matter where I am or what I'm doing—and remember. Remember what's important, and who's important.

My grandparents always knew.

Living by the Seat of his Jeans

My brother Andy has a knack for bringing what I call Andrewisms into my life. Andrewisms are situations and incidents that are too surreal to believe, yet they always seem to happen when he's at the helm. Whether it's accidently setting a car on fire by tying up its tailpipe with wire or taking a divot out of a new kitchen floor while demonstrating his golf swing, Andrewisms are virtually impossible for anyone to achieve but Andy. I'd thought he'd outgrown them with age but when my kids were younger I was reminded quite clearly that he had not.

I must, for the sake of fairness, describe my brother before I try to describe his latest Andrewism. He's supremely intelligent, a technical chemist, and one of the most compassionate people I know. His care and concern for others is so genuine that some don't know what to make of him. He's a deacon in his church, a wonderful husband and a loving father.

He also drives a pickup truck and a Harley Davidson, which he built from scratch himself. He likes hole-in-the-wall bars, mainly because of the conversations he can strike up, and is loath to wear anything but jeans and cowboy boots. He's completely unafraid to be himself, no matter where he is and whom he's with. He's a wonderful brother to have.

However, sometimes when he's involved with a project, things don't quite go as planned. Events somehow go awry. These episodes are what those closest to him call Andrewisms. They're each unique, completely unexpected, and usually costly. So, several years ago when my brother offered to take my two older children fishing for the afternoon, I experienced a genuine twinge of concern. We were visiting Andy and his wife in North Carolina at the time; I wasn't sure where he'd be taking them or what exactly they'd use for bait.

I shrugged it off. Surely, this fishing trip would be safe and kid-appropriate. My brother was now a responsible adult; he was not the same uncle who tried to feed his nine-month-old niece pepperoni and garlic pizza. And my kids worshiped him. They would love an afternoon with Uncle Andy. So, I mentally scolded myself for being overprotective, and helped them get ready for the big fishing trip.

After all, what could happen?

Before I left the house with my sister-in-law—who's a saint, a virtual walking saint—I glanced into the bedroom where my brother was busy wrestling with the kids. My four-year-old son screamed with delight as he was hurled through the air onto the bed, his head missing the steel bedframe by inches. I refused to second-guess my decision to condone the fishing trip and started swiftly for the door.

My hand was on the handle when I heard the wailing. My brother came running into the kitchen with my sobbing son in his arms, looking contrite. He rooted through the freezer for an ice pack and assured me the head was not bleeding and the pupils were not dilated. I bit back a reply and bravely headed to the car.

My sister-in-law and I had a wonderful afternoon browsing through antique shops and arrived home with plans to relax before the fishermen came home with their catch. It had been, we both agreed, a relaxing day without the kids; we had done the right thing by letting my brother entertain them. It was then we noticed the phone blinking and checked the voice messages to hear my brother's voice.

"Hey, we've had a little breakdown here, and we're stranded. We're at the gas station on County Road K. We'll be waiting; can you please get us as soon as you can?" I could dimly hear my daughter's voice chirping in the background but that was all I could discern.

We left to rescue them immediately, and I was more concerned than I cared to admit. It was a 95-degree muggy afternoon. Did they have water? Were the kids scared? Where exactly were they and what had happened?

We found them, minus the truck, at the gas station about 10 miles away. The kids were beaming, brimming with the adventure, and sticky with candy donated by the kind owner of the gas station. They were muddy and covered with scratches to boot. My son's face was streaked with dried tears, but he seemed completely recovered from whatever the trauma had been. We put Andy and the kids in the car and followed the tow truck to my brother's now useless Chevy Pickup.

As we navigated the bumpy country roads, the kids filled us in on the details of their adventure.

"We drove over a big stick in the road, and it broke our tire! We never even got to fish. Then we left the truck and walked and walked but got really thirsty. Then, we were chased by a really mean dog, but Uncle Andy helped us get away. We fell down and Rhett's knee was bleeding, but it feels better now."

Wonderful.

"Then, we had to go to the bathroom, so Uncle Andy told us to use the woods. It was great! We used leaves to wipe."

Super, I replied evenly.

"The thing I'm sad about," confessed my daughter, "is that I never got a chance to drive. I was supposed to drive after Rhett, but when he was driving we ran over the stick and wrecked the tire."

My brother had the grace to look sheepish. "Rhett was doing a fine job," he protested. "He was steering like a champ when the branch came out of nowhere. I looked away for a minute and there it was. There was no way he could have avoided it."

I gazed at him incredulously. Rhett was four. Of course he couldn't have avoided it.

Although I was trying to look stern and disapproving, I realized I probably looked resigned. After all, deep down I'd known an afternoon of uneventful fishing would not occur. I hadn't known what would happen, but I had known what wouldn't – the original plan.

When you think about it, my brother illustrates the story of our lives. He just paints the picture a bit more boldly. Despite our best-laid plans, the unexpected happens. It's how we react to the unexpected that shows our character.

My kids never got to fish. But they were exposed to something more important . . . grace under pressure.

A Family Tradition

Sometimes, in this tumultuous and volatile life, we yearn for stability. We want to know something —anything —is immune to the frenzied pace of today's society. We want to go to this place, rest, and enjoy just being.

We may not think such place exists. But I was there, just last week. And while I was there, time stopped. Nothing mattered but the crack of the ball on the bat, the fans cheering and the organ playing. Wrigley Field is an oasis of calm in the midst of a city teeming with change. It brings you back to a different era, one where players played for the love of the game and modest money, and the only way to follow a Cubs game was to attend or tune in the radio.

My husband took me to the Cubs game for an early Mother's Day present. We sat in the left field bleachers, soaked in the sun and made 20 instant best friends. We screamed with joy when the Cubs got a hit and moaned in despair when the Cardinals hit a grand slam. We sang lustily to the national anthem and waved to the outfielders. We didn't glance at our watches once.

We were in a timeless zone. But for the lights, which weren't on during this afternoon game, Wrigley Field was how it had always been. The ivy was flourishing and the grass was real. The manual scoreboard was still the vocal point of the outfield, and when the score changed, the old number was pulled out and the new number was put in. If you watched carefully, you could see a little head in the empty square during the number changing. The advertisements are slowly creeping onto the sturdy brick walls of Wrigley, but they're still at a minimum compared with other major league ball fields.

Because the park is unchanged, memories abound within it. I couldn't help wondering if my grandfather had ever sat in my exact seat. Perhaps he had. Growing up in the Swedish neighborhood that surrounded Wrigley Field in the 1920's, he never missed a Cubs game if he could help it. He and his buddies made a good buck parking cars, valet-style, for the games. After the first few innings, they would hop the fence surrounding Wrigley and enjoy the Cubs in action until the fans started to leave. Then, they would resume their stations and retrieve the cars.

As a child, I questioned my grandfather extensively on the fence-hopping angle of this story. How did he get over the fence? Which fence was the easiest to climb? Where in the park did he sit, and did he ever get caught not having a ticket stub? My grandfather, I believe realizing his error in divulging too much information, refused to reveal details about his many illegal entries. Suffice it to say he and the neighborhood boys rarely paid to see their team play.

My father remembers his grandfather taking him to Wrigley Field in the 1940's. My great-grandfather owned a restaurant on Sheffield, right by the ball park, and was a Cubs fanatic. With my father—his grandson—in tow, he would go to as many games as he could justify.

He spent countless summer afternoons in the park, screaming in his heavily accented English and having a blast.

Thirty years later, my father started taking my brother and me where his grandfather and father had spent so many afternoons in the sun. I remember those afternoons well. My brother, clutching his mitt, would pray for a foul ball. I would be praying a foul ball wouldn't hit us. We wolfed down hot dogs with everything, peanuts, and more Cokes than we could count. It was during those games in the 70's that I became a Cub fan for life, like the generations before me.

While I was enjoying the game last week, I closed my eyes and watched. I saw my grandfather, a 17-year-old Swedish boy, hop the fence laden with car keys and slip unobtrusively into a seat. I saw him revel in the game, young and strong and laughing. I saw my father as a skinny eight-year-old boy, hoping the Cubs would hit one over the fence, and hoping his grandpa wouldn't embarrass him by screaming too loudly.

I also saw myself behind the third-base line on Jack Brickhouse's last day of announcing with the Cubs. I saw myself cutting out of work early on opening day in 1994, meeting my husband at the park, and freezing for the entire afternoon. Opening day at Wrigley is always artic; when will I ever learn? I remembered going to Wrigley with high school friends, catching a foul ball and giving it to the little boy next to us.

As it always is with life, many things have changed. My great-grandfather, grandfather and Jack Brickhouse are no longer alive. My father and I no longer live in the same state. I don't work downtown anymore, and I probably can no longer catch a foul ball without glasses. So many changes indeed. But Wrigley Field stays the same. It was the only constant in all of my ponderings.

We all need some consistency in our lives, don't we?

Chapter 2: Parenting With Prayer

"For the Christian, parental authority does not come from God placing us over our children. It comes from God having given us the responsibility to serve His children whom He, for a time, has entrusted to our care."

— <u>Greg and Lisa Popcak</u>

The White Caped Crusader

When my son Rhett was in preschool, he became obsessed with a white cape.

I was unfazed, figuring this infatuation would fade with time; say, a few hours. After all, he was four. And four year old boys, though tasty, usually don't have very long attention spans. Redirecting is often and easily done. I considered myself somewhat of a master at this parenting skill, but the white cape was the real thing. Nothing could deter my son's passion or dampen his enthusiasm for this incredible piece of attire.

The love affair with the cape began after an afternoon of playing with his best friend. Rhett came home with a radiant countenance, bursting with details about a white cape.

It was white (really?), flowing, and transforming. It was the most beautiful cape ever made, and if you chose, you could also add the mask that matched the cape. This mask disguised the wearer so well you'd never guess he was really a kid. When the cape and mask were donned, you became a super hero who could save the entire world from the bad guys. Since more super heroes were needed in the world, Rhett earnestly explained, I needed to get him a white cape, pronto. He had work to do, and he couldn't do it without the powers of a white cape.

My son went to bed talking about the white cape. He woke up talking about the white cape. He pleaded to invite himself over to his friend's house so he could wear the cape again. He took sheets and towels and attempted to pin them around his neck. He sat in his booster chair and spoke wistfully about how powerful he was when he wore the cape. I heard about the magical cape for three days straight. Finally, I caved. I told him I'd call his friend's mother to see where she bought it.

"She didn't buy it," my son told me. "She made it herself!" My hand dropped away from the telephone. Made it? I can barely sew on a button, I thought. How did she have time to make it? She worked part time and had three children, just like me. I threw myself on the mercy of my neighbors and borrowed Batman and Superman capes, presenting them to my son with much ceremony. No dice. "Mommy," he said patiently, "these capes are not white and they do not have masks. They don't disguise me! I need to wear the magical white cape to be the kind of super hero I want to be."

One day my son floated home from preschool and announced the news. His friend had brought the cape and mask to school and allowed my son to borrow it. With a flourish, he unzipped his backpack and pulled out a bridal veil.

Upon closer inspection, it only looked like a bridal veil. It was of course, the cape, made from tulle. Tulle? The top was rolled into a circle that a boy shoved over his head, and voilá! A cape. The clever, disguising mask was a small piece of tulle that tied around the wearer's eyes and nose, reminding me of the Lone Ranger at the marriage alter. No sewing was involved.

But a parent was. Time and listening was. A mother slowed down and entered a child's world. An extra piece of tulle was manipulated to make two little boys ecstatically happy. This rolled up piece of fabric, in my son's four-year-old eyes, blew the shiny store-bought Superman and Batman capes away. The white cape was magic because a parent created it just for them. No money was spent, but watching four-year-olds transform themselves into super heroes was priceless.

We need to remember that the best thing we can give our children —besides a love of Christ — is ourselves. That's all they really want.

I was pondering this as I was driving with my son the next day, yet at the same time, I was also stressing about the week ahead of me: a column due and not started, a meeting at church that would not offer childcare, a bible study to teach, and a preschool fieldtrip to chaperone. Plus, I was down to my last three diapers. I could feel my jaw clenching and my neck tightening when Rhett tapped my shoulder. "Mommy," he said, "I wish we could go to the library today. I would love to look at some dinosaurs." I opened my mouth to refuse this simple request, and explain that mommy was very busy and we would have to go another day. Then I thought of the cape and the joy it brought, executed a rather reckless U-turn that made my son squeal with joy, and headed for the library.

We spent an hour there together, just my son and me, trying to find the dinosaur book with the scariest illustrations showcasing the most teeth. After we made our selection, we went to the park and read. As I was struggling to pronounce the name of an intelligent, nest-making dinosaur, I felt a small arm snake around my waist. I stopped reading to savor the moment. Right then, sitting on a park bench with my boy, my heart was full. I needed nothing more.

And neither did he.

The rewards of slowing down for your children are sweet. At the very least, you'll understand your God-given power as a parent. Anything, even a leftover piece of tulle, can become exciting. Anywhere, even a stone bench, can be a great place to cuddle. Children's needs and wants are simple, but they do take our time. I'm not sure where I'll gain some extra time. But I do know I must, no matter how old they're getting.

It took me two days to coax my son out of the white cape. He'd been joyfully running around the house looking like a deranged bride. We'd had enough, and the cape's owner had been patiently awaiting its return. Rhett's honeymoon with the cape was short and sweet, but while it lasted, it was true love.

The Card

One late summer day, I was brought back to college with a start.

For an afternoon, I was no longer a wife, mother of three, dog and guinea pig owner, and writer. I was eighteen, sitting in my dorm room, waiting for The Knock.

The Knock would signify the end of an agonizing three-month process. The Knock would map out the remainder of my college career. The Knock would bring one of two results – exaltation or devastation.

I remember how I felt waiting for that knock. The clock ticked with agonizing slowness. My heart stopped every time I heard footsteps in the hall. When The Knock finally came, I almost ripped the door off its hinges. An envelope was handed to me, wishes of luck were murmured, and the knocker was gone. I ripped open the envelope to learn my sorority bid had been accepted; I was cordially invited to pledge the Delta Chi Theta sorority.

Joy and relief flooded through me. I screamed with delight, and then ran for the phone. Who was in my pledge class with me? What had my friend's envelopes told them? I couldn't wait to hear the good news; surely, this would be a wonderful celebratory evening for all of us.

The next few hours were bittersweet. I had many overjoyed friends, and many who were crushed. Some were crying with joy;

others in despair. Some swore they were transferring schools; some were clutching their bids tightly to their breasts. The girls I was closest to had pledged different sororities, and when I walked into the room to meet my pledge class there were only a few familiar faces. The original college crowd was being disbanded and rearranged. On the heels of my initial joy was genuine discomfort. Things were changing, new people were coming into the mix, and everything was not as it should have been.

These emotions, which I hadn't examined in many years, came flooding back on an August day. That day, children in our neighborhood got the equivalent of The Knock. They got The Card.

These bright orange cards ended months of suspense, hope and worry for hundreds of elementary school children and their parents. They determined who the recipient would do projects with, have recess with and eat lunch with each day for an entire school year. The Card revealed teacher assignments.

As a novice to the elementary school experience, I didn't quite grasp the power of The Card. The day of The Card's arrival, I walked in the house and checked my phone messages. There were nine. Considering we'd only been gone about an hour, I was surprised. For the first time, I glanced down at the mail I had carried in. The Card was on top, in all its glory. The identity of my daughter's teacher was finally known.

I checked the messages. Most centered around The Card. Just as we did when we were invited to pledge, everyone wanted to know who was going where. The first three messages were from my daughter's best friend. The next three were from assorted friends. The next one was from a mother who didn't get The Card in her mail that day and was thinking it got lost in the mail; she was calling the school. The next was from a distraught mother proclaiming she was calling the principal about her son's teacher assignment. The last one was from my husband, blissfully unaware of The Card and asking if the gutter estimate had arrived yet.

The day slowly sorted itself out. Little by little we identified who was – and wasn't – in my daughter's first grade class. Tears were shed, squeals of delight issued. Talks were conducted stressing new friends were wonderful, and old friends were everlasting. By the day's end, my daughter was perfectly content, and I was emotionally exhausted.

The Card is a part of our children's lives we can't control; that's why it rocks our world when it arrives. And if we think about it, it's a vital reminder that we are not ultimately in charge, not of our own lives, and not of our children's. Hard as this is to grasp, it's a very good thing. God is in control, and he's smarter than us.

Many years ago, I thought I knew why I was pledging a sorority. I thought I knew what the experience would do for me. As it turned out, it did nothing I thought it would and many things I never imagined it could. That's the way it is with so many things in life. We're confident we know our destination, and we can determine how we'll get there. As we grow wiser, in our faith and in ourselves, we understand that's not the case.

Sometimes this realization is scary. More and more often for me, it's becoming strangely comforting.

After all, I've got enough on my plate.

Color Blind

As we walked through the Abraham Lincoln's house in Springfield, Illinois, I watched my children soak up history like little sponges. My two oldest, going into second grade and fourth grade, seemed especially excited about walking up the same staircase Abe Lincoln had used while a state senator. My son Rhett, who eschewed school and organized learning of any kind, ran his little hand over the banister and whispered, reverently, "Can you believe Abraham Lincoln's hand was on this same wood?" His eyes were shining. I thought again about what a great idea it was to take this trip to our state capital, especially for Rhett. He was soaking up the living history with an attention span I didn't know he possessed. I was greatly encouraged.

We stayed at a hotel that night, further adding to the children's joy. What was better than an indoor swimming pool and free sugar coated cereal at the breakfast bar in the morning? My mother and I watched the kids in the pool while we plotted out the next day. We decided to spend the day at the Abraham Lincoln Museum, which was highly touted as a wonderful exploration of the life and impact of Illinois' most famous president.

The next morning, fueled by unlimited and usually forbidden Fruit Loops, the kids started their museum adventure. The museum was extremely kid friendly and interactive, and the kids loved it as much as they had loved touring Lincoln's home. One of the most memorable and sobering exhibits was the life-size depiction of a slave auction. This exhibit was horrifying in its emotion, clearly portraying the sorrow and anguish in a slave mother's face as her child was being sold to the highest bidder. The mother in chains was reaching out for her child, unable to save him as he was being led away. The exhibit was extremely well done and very disturbing to view, but I knew it was important that my children really understood the evils of slavery. The life-size depiction of the slave mother and child said more to my children than any history book ever could.

There were many more exhibits concerning slavery, but none stayed with me as clearly as the auction portrayal of the mother and child. My knees literally felt weak as I imagined myself in that mother's place.

That night we went out for our last dinner in Springfield. As we sat around the table we recapped the day, especially the slavery exhibits. My oldest daughter mentioned how glad she was that we hailed from Illinois, the Land of Lincoln. We all agreed Illinois had a history we could be proud of. Then my eight year old son spoke up. "Boy, wouldn't it have been horrible to live in the south while there were slaves? Imagine if we were alive back then and didn't live in Illinois, but in a southern state!"

We agreed with him that living in the south during the Civil War would have been dicey at best. I wasn't quite sure what he was driving at and tried to help him formulate his thoughts. "You mean we would have been different than other southerners by refusing to own slaves?

Or do you mean some of us probably would have been killed in the war?" Rhett shook his head impatiently.

"No! I mean we could have been slaves! It would be horrible to be a slave!"

I stared at him, a bit unsure on which way to jump. "Buddy," I said, "why do you think we might have been slaves back then?"

Rhett gave us all a disbelieving look. "If we lived in the South, we might have been slaves! Some southern people were slaves! No northern people were slaves. Sheesh! You know this from the museum."

My mother, older daughter and I had stopped eating and were gaping at him. My youngest daughter was focused on drawing on the paper placement and had stopped tracking the conversation.

I found my voice. "Rhett, we wouldn't have been slaves back then. Think about what we just saw at the museum. What did the slaves look like? Did they look like you?"

Rhett looked puzzled. "Well, there was a boy about my age in that auction exhibit," he clarified.

My older daughter could stand it no longer. "Rhett, the slaves were African American, not white like you! African American people were the slaves! How could you not know this?" She exhaled in disgust and rolled her eyes to heaven. "Man, we went through that entire museum and you weren't paying attention!"

My heart was swelling, because I knew he had been paying attention. Rapt attention. He just didn't see. He did not notice, in a hall full of hundreds of pictures, paintings and life size exhibits, that the slaves had a certain color skin. He did not see it.

It was sad to see his face change as he processed this new information. He looked stunned, confused and unhappy. "You mean all the slaves were African American?"

I affirmed that they were and then followed up with a question that had an obvious answer. I just wanted to hear it voiced. "Rhett, didn't you notice that in the exhibits all the slaves had dark skin?"

He looked at me in genuine discomfort. "No. I didn't."

He really didn't.

That dinner will forever remain in my memory. It was my realization of — yet sadly also the end of — my son's innocence. I loved him for literally not noticing skin color and believing that God created us all in love and equal. I loved him for the disbelief that flickered over his face when he realized that to some people in this broken world, skin color matters. I love that as a teenager he still remains as color-blind as the world will allow him to be.

It's hard to watch our children's faces fall as they recognize evil in this world, but it's uplifting as they decide to fight against that evil. We need to remember to encourage them with prayer and instruction every step of the way.

Growing Pains

N
ow that I'm parenting three children, I'm praying more than ever. Perhaps you can relate to this strategy. I'm asking God especially for wisdom and discernment in what I expose my children to, and when. How much reality is too much, too soon? What's the difference between helicopter parenting and being a responsible parent? I don't know these answers, but the good news is God does. I know He'll help me if I ask Him, and I really need guidance through this uncharted territory. The first time I really remember struggling with too much, too soon was when my daughter was in first grade. Little did I know it was the beginning of many similar discussions to come.

My then eight-year-old daughter came in from school, kicked off her boots, and started rooting through her backpack. "Mom, it was library day today," she announced. "I got two new books!"

She pulled out the first book with a flourish. "Look!" she crowed. I glanced over at it while changing a diaper. It was a Magic Tree House Book. Good enough. I knew she loved that series. Then she held out the second book for inspection. "This one is going to be really great. It's got tons of really cool pictures in it." I cut my eyes toward the book while snapping my toddler's jeans. I froze, then released my youngest and watched her trot off. "Let me look at that book again," I requested.

My daughter handed over <u>Anne Frank: Beyond the Diary</u>, for my perusal. She immediately detected my hesitation. "Mom, I know you think this book is too old for me, but I already know what it's all about. In fact, I know what happened to the girl on the cover."

I tried to recall how old I was when I read the story of Anne Frank. Fourth grade, maybe? Definitely not first grade, of that I was sure. My heart sank. How did she already know of this horror story? What exactly did she know?

I drew a deep breath. "What do you know about Anne Frank?" I asked calmly. "Everything!" my daughter stated authoritatively. "I know she lived a long time ago, and she was a servant in the attic of a big house. She hid there for a while and put lots of pictures on the walls. The house is even still there! I think I'm old enough to know about that."

I exhaled slowly. "Well, if you want to read this book you may, but we must read it together. There are some things in this book that I'll need to explain to you, like religious persecution." I noted my daughter's eyes were beginning to glaze over. "Maybe I'll just read the Magic Tree House book right now," she said. She hooked an apple and her book and went to her secret reading spot (that the entire family knew about). I was grateful for the temporary reprieve.

Oddly enough, my husband and I had just visited the Anne Frank House during our autumn trip to Amsterdam. Although I had read The Diary of Anne Frank as a girl and knew quite a bit about the Holocaust, I was unprepared for the raw emotion that flooded me during the tour. Walking through the Frank family's hiding place brings home the desperateness and horror of that time in a way books and documentaries just can't.

There's something piercing about stepping over the very threshold Anne stepped over, standing in the room she slept in, and climbing the stairs she descended to her final doom. Gazing at the magazine pictures she pasted on the walls to brighten her dreary years of seclusion moved me to tears. As a parent, I kept putting myself in the place of Anne's parents, trying valiantly to save my children from the hands of Nazi soldiers. The agony of Anne's father, the only survivor in the family, was clearly portrayed in video interviews at the end of the tour. I literally staggered out of the building; the sheer horror of the Frank family's experience was almost too much to comprehend.

These thoughts were galloping through my mind as I gazed at the abandoned library book on the floor. I scooped it up and leafed through it. The book had dozens of photographs of Anne and her family in happier days, and only a few of the concentration camps. There were pictures of Jewish people in lines wearing the required stars, and some of the house Anne and her family lived in secretly for two years. No images were overtly graphic or disturbing at first glance. I knew I'd have to read through it carefully before I could make any sort of decision regarding its appropriateness.

I realized this was the beginning of many agonizing decisions I'd be forced to make as my children grew older. Was this book appropriate for my daughter to read, even with me at her side? Or should I let her remain — for the moment — a true child, secure in the fact that with her parents on guard, nothing could harm her? As my kids have grown, I've had to grapple with the issue of parental censorship more and more. What movies should be forbidden? Which websites? How often should I monitor their text messages and Facebook pages? These quandaries are commonplace now, yet that Anne Frank book remains, in my mind, a crystal-clear image of the first time I grappled with the problem of too much, too soon.

I never had to make a decision about that book, because my daughter was not thrilled about reading anything with me. If she had to read it with me she wasn't interested. She wanted to read herself, not because she wasn't a loving child, but because she finally could. So, the Anne Frank book temporarily lost its appeal.

But it would be back. And it would be the first of many books, movies and websites I'd have to screen, assess, and permit or forbid. After all, my children would keep growing. And that is a blessing some parents, including Otto Frank, do not always have.

I must remember to not only ask the Lord for guidance while raising my children, but also to continually give thanks to Him for those very children. They are gifts from Him, and every day with them is a blessing.

Rain on the Roof

One day, as we were sitting together in the kitchen, my son surprised me by articulating a theological truth. He threw it out casually as he leafed through his Algebra book. I looked up from my laptop and blinked. What did he just say? And where did it come from? "You're absolutely right," I praised him. "How did you know that?"

"I heard it," he replied. This terse response didn't surprise me. Getting information out of my son often resembles a major archeological dig. Yes — he'll blithely say, when I can't stand it anymore and call his cell phone — he made the basketball team. Why didn't he call and tell me as soon as he found out? He didn't think of it, sorry.

I mentally prepared myself for slowly and carefully extracting the information I was seeking.

"Well, where did you hear it?" This question, I figured, would have to be repeated in four different ways to be answered. But the answer would come, I was sure of it.

I was shocked when the answer came immediately. He looked at me and sighed, exasperated. "I heard it from you!" he stated rather impatiently. "Remember, on my bed, when we were talking about this?"

"Of course I remember," I quickly assured him. "I just wondered if you remembered."

This answer, I must confess, was not brimming with truth. I did, rather fuzzily, remember the bedtime conversation he referenced. But I didn't remember saying anything remotely like the truth he just uttered. In fact, sitting on my children's beds at the day's end was not my cognitive shining time; I was usually so dazed with tiredness myself that I had to fight to stay awake while I tucked them in. That I said anything worth remembering was a first. I was stunned, once again, about how completely our kids soak us up.

They digest what we say, what we do, and how we act. They adopt our mannerisms, our inflections, and our viewpoints. They are always – perpetually— listening. I was thrilled my son had remembered such an edifying nugget from our conversation. I was also a little nervous when I pondered how many things he might remember me saying that were not edifying.

Our tongues are very powerful, and, especially with our children, very influential. Proverbs 15:4 clearly reminds us, *"The tongue that brings healing is a tree of life, but a deceitful tongue crushes the spirit."* We can all probably remember statements or observations made by our parents that they have no recollection of voicing. In their minds, these verbalized thoughts were perhaps mundane, or route. To us, when we were children, they were gospel.

I remember one comment my Dad made almost thirty years ago. I even remember where we were when he said it. We were traveling south on West Street, and had just passed the cemetery. It was raining hard. My father commented how much he loved the sound of rain on the car roof, and how safe and snug it made him feel. From that time on, that has always been my opinion of rain on my car roof. As a seven-year-old I absorbed that thought and have never released it.

Ordinary as that memory is, it illustrates the power of a parent. What we say means something. What we say is remembered, and can be tucked away in a child's memory for the rest of his life. We need to be diligent with our words, and just as importantly, our tone. At times, that can be a rough task indeed; some days are better than others. In fact, some years are better than others.

Something else to ponder: Why, if they're so absorbed with our words, do kids seem to have selective hearing? How could my son digest an advanced (for him) theological truth and restate it perfectly, yet seem unable to follow my directives to make his bed? It is, I confess, a true mystery, one that continues to this day. He can remember basketball plays till the cows come home, but remembering to turn in his math homework seems to be quite a challenge. Interesting.

My son's comment that day made me a bit contemplative about choosing words, but for the most part it energized me. I was excited that my children were listening. I'm not sure if they always will. In fact, I'm certain there will be times in their lives that they won't. I remember several years during which I listened to very little of what my parents said. Now, I listen to everything they say once again.

Parents aren't perfect. Ours weren't, and we aren't. But we do have security in the perfection of our heavenly father. He makes no mistakes. And everything written in His book is perfect. When we're groping for what to say and what not to say, we should always reference His words. And, we should encourage our kids to do the same, especially as they grow older and enter into situations that may be scary or tempting. Fall back on scripture. It won't steer us wrong.

My father has sheepishly admitted he has no recollection of his rain-on-the-roof comment. But he seems pleased I remember it. A bit puzzled, but pleased.

Social Stresses

Years ago, when I was the proud mother of a newborn, a two-year-old and a four-year-old, I thought parenting couldn't get any tougher. Every day was a blur of care-taking, feeding and physical lifting. Merely strapping the three kids in the car ate up ten minutes, and this was after the twenty-minute prelude of coats and shoes. When well-meaning mothers of older children assured me I would look back on those days with yearning, I bit my tongue and smiled. Obviously, they were still mentally challenged from the years I was currently in the midst of. In time, they would recover. Perhaps I would too.

When my daughter entered first grade, I was confident the hardest parenting days were behind me. After all, my children were now becoming more independent – no one was in diapers and one was in elementary school full time. I was looking forward to easier days to come. However, in one eye-opening morning, I saw, for the first time, that the steepness of the parenting road was increasing each and every year. I thought I had attained level ground, and was stunned to realize my climb was just beginning.

My revelation began when I volunteered to chaperone a walking field trip. When I arrived in my daughter's classroom, the teacher was assigning partners. The rule was they had to walk in twos, preferably holding hands. Even a novice like me could immediately detect the importance of the partner selection. The room was absolutely silent as the teacher would call out a name, hesitate, and then call out the second. Faces would light up or fall, muffled cheers or groans were detectable. Some children went up to the teacher to negotiate a more acceptable walking partner. To the teacher's credit, she didn't budge, but I began to feel slightly stressed.

When the partners were standing together in an orderly line, we set off down the sidewalk. That's when my enlightenment began.

Kids immediately started boycotting their partners. They hung back pretending to tie a shoe or zip a coat, or they'd run forward on the pretense they needed to relay important information to someone and "forget" to come back to their partner. In the blink of an eye, some kids were walking alone while others were walking in threes. Some girls who were not partners had their arms around each other, others who were partners would not look at each other. I watched one girl yank her hand out of another's and wipe it on her pants. When I called her on it, she gave me a blinding smile and assured me her hand was just sweaty; she'd love to hold her partner's hand again. In the time it took to walk eight blocks, I had a disheartening preview of the many social traumas in years to come.

Of course, I tried my best to fix things. I found myself dashing back and forth, nipping at heels like an overzealous Border Collie. "Zack, you move back to Tyler, he's your partner." "Taylor, remember to hold hands with Grace, your partner. Ellie already has a partner."

"Emma is walking alone; who's Emma's partner?" "Charlie, you do not trip your partner. You walk with you partner nicely." It was an exhausting endeavor.

Despite these efforts, there were still children walking alone or feeling left out. I found myself walking with them chatting determinedly, trying to distract and soothe. But I have to admit, although my efforts may have helped, they didn't fix anything. The kids who weren't wanted as partners knew they weren't wanted, even as I pranced about in an attempt to repair things. These children were now socially on their own, at least during school hours. Sometimes they'd come home with their feelings hurt and their wings clipped. Sometimes they'd come home buoyant feeling popular and accepted. As hard as it is for parents, we cannot control this.

And that realization can be harder than all the diaper changing in the world.

Although having young children is hard, it's more physically than mentally challenging. You're always busy, but you're also still in charge (or you think you are) of their social interactions. You arrange play times with other children you know. If there's a dispute, you rush in, soothe, and make it right. Play dates are often arranged around the mothers' relationships rather than children's friendships. And, perhaps most importantly, when children are very young, they almost always play one-on-one. That way, no one is left out. But as we know, parents can't negotiate friendships forever.

It's hard to watch any child struggle with friendships and acceptance, but our faith can help us here. We need to remember that God is in control, and since He created our children, there's no one more qualified to guide them. We simply cannot parent alone, and we should give thanks that we don't have to. He will help us through every stage and give us the strength we need to step back. And He will always be our children's partner. They'll never have to walk alone.

Chapter 3: Natural Thoughts

The best remedy for those who are afraid, lonely or unhappy is to go outside, somewhere where they can be quiet, alone with the heavens, nature and God.
*—**Anne Frank** - The Diary*
(12 June 1942 - 1 August 1944)

The Bee Dance

I've always been terrified of bees.

When I was little, my fear bordered on hysteria. I was so scared of bees or the possibility of bees that I spent a lot of time inside on beautiful summer days. When I ventured outside and a bee did fly near me I'd emit a blood-curdling scream and start flailing about, swinging blindly at the bee while attempting to run the other way. My mother would roll her eyes and tell me to calm down and freeze. If I would freeze, she insisted, I wouldn't get stung.

I look back at my childhood bee behavior and cringe. I was truly out of control; no wonder I kept getting stung. Now, as a sensible adult and mother, I've modified my actions. Now I don't scream at all.

The rest I continue to do. My daughter rolls her eyes and says, "Mom, the teachers at school tell us to just freeze! Freeze! Stop moving your arms."

I've come full circle.

But in my defense, bees are everywhere these days. I'm certain bees were not this prominent when I was a kid, because I would have been a hysterical wreck every August and September. Each year there seems to be more of these "sweat bees," the common name for almost everything that stings and is not a honeybee.

When I searched Google for information about sweat bees, I wanted to know two things: Why their numbers seem to be increasing, and how to kill them. Instead, I pulled up articles and papers raving about the benefits of these horrid bees. They are so beneficial for pollination, I read, that we should be thankful for their increased numbers. And, one researcher gushed; their social development is extremely interesting. They are usually solitary creatures, though occasionally two females will share an underground tunnel.

Who cares? Has everyone lost their minds? These pesky things make any sort of outdoor activity torture for months. I kept searching.

The next site I found showed a sweat bee nestling prettily in the center of a beautiful yellow flower. Well, call me crazy, but I've never seen a sweat bee on a flower, only a pop can, a playground or a soccer field. The site went on to say that when the bees do sting it's the person's fault for brushing them away (they're usually gentle, compassionate creatures). The sting is not serious, and barely hurts according to three different web sites. If the bees are left alone, the sites insist, they will leave you alone.

My research project was not a success, so I created my own opinionated answers to my two unanswered questions: no one cares why their numbers have increased; and, you can't kill them; there are too many. Don't even try. Also, don't use any soap, deodorant, shampoo, perfume, lotion, hairspray, lip gloss or anything with any fragrance at all. If you do, you're fussing the bees and it's just deserts if you get stung. In fact, if you can roll in mud before you venture outside you'll be ahead of the game.

As I've found no solution to beating back the sweat bees, I continue to do my bee dance each day. My most successful ruse is swatting the bee down and quickly stepping on it. This is not my nature. I catch spiders in my bathroom and release them outside. I shimmy down deep window wells to rescue stranded snakes and toads. I've always taught my children to respect all living things because God created them. I've also taken other children gently aside (to the embarrassment of my own) to explain that tearing the wings of a butterfly hurts it and stepping on a worm because you can is cruel. I simply cannot abide harming something minding its own business and just being itself. Alarmingly, I'm caught in a lesson of my own making.

My daughter, while observing me grinding a downed bee into the pavement, became righteous. "Mom, you can't do that! It didn't sting you — you just hit it out of the air as it flew around. It wasn't touching you at all! God made that bee! You can't just kill it!"

"Bees don't count," I answered grimly, swatting in the air for my next victim.

"But Mom! If bees are alive God made them, and you're hurting something God made! You always tell us we can't do that. Why don't bees count?"

"I'm not sure," I replied, still flailing. "We'll go home and call Grandpa. He'll explain."

My father, a retired pastor, is increasingly my fall guy. I refer all the impossible theological kid questions to him. He is gracious about it, but this bee query might make him a bit edgy.

But I'm edgy enough that anyone else is fair game.

The upside of the bee swarms is my kids are not afraid of them. They treat them like flies, ignoring them almost completely. When my youngest was two she had already been stung four times, and was seemingly impervious to their stings. She refused to be driven away from a snack or drink by the bees; she'd actually fight them for it. She was so little, and the bees so numerous, I sometimes worried they'd pick her up and carry her away.

The fight between the bees and small children is always exasperated by well-meaning parents bringing Dunkin Donuts and juice boxes to morning soccer games and popsicles to share on the playground. In my mind, this is equivalent to breaking out a bag of peanuts in front of seagulls on the beach. Never a good idea.

There is one upside to the bees swarms for me as well. Instead of grieving the end of summer, I've started to eagerly embrace a nice crisp fall and a nice early frost. Who cares about the end of long, warm sunny days filled with pools and picnics? Who needs the early morning chirping of the birds and the delightful hours of gardening? Fall, and long, hard, frozen winters sound pretty good. I'll venture outside once again, decked out in fragrance and hairspray and not afraid. I'll even bring a sugary drink outside, simply because I can. I'll just have to drink it quickly before it freezes.

Crab Complexities

It seems at times that life's simplest pleasures are getting more complicated. Pet ownership is the perfect example.

My childhood dog was fed and walked. Once a year he went to the vet. Today, I am a golden retriever owner, groomer, and canine pharmacy. Twice daily, I measure out natural pet food to combat allergies. I dispense Benadryl three times a day wrapped in cheese, also for aforementioned allergies. I clip toenails and brush fur. I clean ears and administer heartworm pills and flea medication each month. Table scraps, the mainstay of my childhood dog, are strictly forbidden.

Don't misunderstand me; I absolutely love my dog and will do anything for him (clearly!). But I just don't remember my childhood dog getting this red-carpet treatment. He'd often have to bark until we remembered to feed him his Gaines Burgers.

Obviously, dog care has become more sophisticated, and I'm okay with that. But combined with the care of an outdoor rabbit and a very demanding guinea pig, I'm at my limit. Still, I gave the green light to two land hermit crabs for my daughter Grace's ninth birthday. They were given to her by two friends; the mothers had called to ensure hermit crabs wouldn't send me screaming into the night. I assured them that hermit crabs were fine; I had several when I was a girl and knew they took very little care.

I had also owned a cat, and at various times, snakes, crayfish, freshwater fish, gerbils, toads and tadpoles. My mother was surprisingly tolerant of this menagerie, and except for the time the gerbil went down the drainpipe, things went smoothly. I enjoyed all these creatures but my land hermit crabs were probably my favorites. These little guys were friendly, interesting to look at and extremely easy to care for.

Hermit crabs are fascinating creations because of what they lack – their own hard shell. Unlike many of their cousins, hermit crabs have soft bodies, and are completely defenseless against predators. They rectify this shortcoming by adopting empty shells from other creatures, usually snails. They fit themselves neatly inside, and block the entrance with their larger claw. When they outgrow their homes they move into new ones. Hermit crabs live in the ocean, and strangely enough, also on land.

Land hermit crabs make great pets. Unlike goldfish, they last, and unlike gerbils, they don't escape. They don't make any mess. They don't bark, dig or claw at the furniture. They cost only a few dollars and eat peanut butter and drink water. You need sand, a few spare shells for housing variety, and plastic container to put them in. Hermit crab ownership is a breeze.

Or it used to be. Things have apparently changed.

When Grace got her hermit crabs at her birthday party she was thrilled. The girls all took turns holding them and watching them come in and out of their shells. They were a huge hit. I was a bit puzzled that the crabs came with special hermit crab food but shook some in the little shell that served as a dish and thought no more about it. The next day Grace researched land hermit crab care on the Internet, and came to me with a long list of concerns regarding her new pets.

First, she wanted me to know that my childhood hermit crabs had suffered greatly under my care. This was due to many reasons which she would now try to explain to me.

Apparently, hermit crabs prefer a varied diet (so do I, but somehow I keep eating the same Zone Bars for breakfast), one high in calcium for molting. Eggshells, strawberries and ground beef should supplement the expensive hermit crab food sold at pet stores. Peanut butter is not encouraged. I thought about pointing out what crabs eat naturally, but refrained.

I was also informed they are very social and must be with several counterparts to be well-adjusted. And, they must have weekly baths. A bath consists of a shallow bowl of lukewarm water in which the crabs can crawl for 20 minutes at a time. Apparently, this refreshes them. After their bath, they can again focus on the intense responsibilities of being crabs.

The renewed crabs must be placed back in their cage of full sand, scraped smooth so they can rearrange it at will. Each night, a responsible crab owner should smooth out the sand to maximize their crab's daily enjoyment.

Finally, an incubator must be purchased for molting crabs. Unfortunately, when hermit crabs molt they are in grave danger of being attacked by the companions they must have for their own happiness. So, they need to be isolated in incubators to shed their skin leisurely, without fear. How one would know exactly when the hermit crab would molt was unclear.

Looking at my anxious daughter broke my heart. It seems like nothing, even owning a land hermit crab, is allowed to be simple. When I was Grace's age, I used to stare at my hermit crabs for long periods of time, enjoying their eyes on stalks and their different colored claws. I liked how their feelers would tap the air, and marveled at how they could hang almost entirely out of their shells without ever falling out.

I told my daughter we would indeed vary her hermit crabs' diet with fruit and found a shallow pan to use for the baths, but I drew the line at the incubator and suggested to her that she did not need to worry about smoothing the sand. I want her to enjoy God's simple creatures for what they are – simple creatures. They don't need expensive care; they just need to be crabs.

I worry that in today's frantic Internet age we have forgotten to enjoy simple living things because we're frantically searching our virtual world. I'm not sure what the cure for this is; but I do know that I will be praying from Psalm 46:10 for my children: *"Be still, and know that I am God."*

Grace is enjoying her hermit crabs and to my relieved delight, she is learning to be still. She'll lie on her stomach and watch them haul across the floor of her room, admiring their beady eyes and laughing at how quickly they slam back into their shells. And, one did molt, even without an incubator. It was fascinating to see.

So often we're moving too fast to see skins shed and new creatures emerge. We need to remember to be still, and simply watch God's creation.

The Turtles

As we pulled into our driveway we were greeted by a turtle resting in our front garden. The kids went into paroxysms of joy, and I was pretty excited myself. Anyone who knows me understands that almost any creature, domestic or wild, brings me great pleasure. I feel animals truly showcase the creativity and sense of humor of our God.

We rushed over to inspect the turtle and found, to our astonishment, that she was laying eggs in our garden. She had evacuated a perfectly round hole in the soil, backed up close to it, and was depositing rubbery looking eggs into it. After each egg popped out from under her tail and dropped neatly in the hole, she tamped some soil on top of it before laying the next. The tamping entailed stretching her back leg to surreal lengths, then retracting it back to normal length for the next egg drop. We got the Flip and videoed the event, complete with close ups of the turtle's rear end. She glared at us in disbelief but never faltered in her task. We had to leave before she was finished but we counted eight eggs before our departure.

When we returned home later that evening every trace of the turtle was gone. The hole was covered; even the woodchips were spread back on top of the hole. It was as though the egg event had never happened.

I researched turtles of the Midwest and quickly determined our turtle was a painted turtle. All websites agreed painted turtle eggs have a 45-

60 day gestation period, though very rarely they could take as long as 90 days. Conservation websites pointed out the best thing to do was to fence in the area with chicken wire as the hatching date approached. That way, you kept the turtles contained until you could get them safely back to water. The sites also suggested ways to keep hungry foxes and raccoons from digging up the eggs, but I drew the line on that. Nature is nature, after all. If the eggs were meant to survive they would survive.

As the eggs were laid on June 15th I figured I should erect my chicken wire by the end of July. The wire did detract from the French Country garden I was trying to coax along, but I was so excited about my baby turtles that I didn't care. Each morning I rushed out to check that: 1. the eggs weren't raided and eaten and 2. the eggs hadn't hatched overnight. Every morning the dirt was undisturbed.

45 days passed. Then 60. Bible study started in the fall and when asked by our small group leader to relate a spiritual highlight of my summer, I talked about the turtle eggs. They were due to hatch any time, and I promised a report when they did.

Then 90 days passed. Then 150. I took down the chicken wire; there was obviously no need for it.

Then it was winter.

In my 43 years I had never experienced such a dismal and frustrating time. I was sick with constant sinus infections and persistent vertigo that sapped my concentration – I would forget what I was saying mid-sentence and often grope for words. My left eye would sometimes swell shut for no apparent reason. I was mired in depression, some days feeling as though I was barely hanging on. And I was always – perpetually — tired. When I would lie down to sleep (sometimes in the middle of the day) it felt as though I was falling down a very deep hole – but I would pass out before I hit the bottom. It only took me about 20 dizzying seconds to fall asleep those gray days. And gray they were. The sun refused to shine that winter; on the rare occasions it did I would find and curl up in a sun patch on my floor. I'd have to fight my retriever for the patch, but I usually won.

As spring approached and the weather thawed I began, rather tentatively, to climb out from the hole I had been in all winter. It was a slow climb but the ascent was certain. Things were getting better; the sun was shining and my dizziness was slowly abating, but my heart was bruised and my usual optimism was at a very low ebb.

Holy Week arrived and with it some warmer sunny days that were a blessing. On Holy Saturday, my daughter and her friend were playing outside when they came running up to me with a muddy quarter. At least, I thought it was a quarter. Upon closer inspection, it was a baby turtle.

A perfect little baby turtle with a scalloped shell, little toenails and a striped face. I was dumbfounded, and then ecstatic — a nest somewhere had survived! Ours had not, but it didn't matter, because another one did! I shouted to the girls to search for more baby turtles, and within minutes we had collected 8 little shells. We placed them in a Pyrex baking dish with some marsh water (my husband quickly drove down the block to grab some) and marveled at their beauty. As they swam, the mud that encrusted them fell away and we could really see how perfectly God designed them.

It was then my husband said, "I can't believe how long these took to hatch! It's a miracle." I stared at him.

"These didn't come from our nest," I admonished him. "Ours never made it." To prove my point, I gestured to our original nest site.

There was a perfectly round hole at the top of it. As we watched, another tiny turtle clawed his way out.

With God's help, we can climb out of our holes. It may take a while, it may seem like we'll never see the light, but we can do it. When we emerge, we may be covered in mud, but that too will wash away with Christ.

We took pictures and invited neighbors to view our treasures, then released them into the marsh. Erring on the side of caution, we left the Pyrex dish over to hole to contain any late stragglers. The last hatchling emerged on Easter morning, covered in mud yet ready to live.

Just like all of us.

Robin Ruminations

A
fter much agonizing, my husband and I traded in our old and charming farmhouse with no room to a sixties brick rectangle with loads of room. It had taken us several years to bite the bullet, but bite it we had. Now, we owned the brick rectangle and there was no going back. As we pulled in ahead of the moving van, we gazed at the front entry. To say it had no charm was an understatement.

"Well," my husband said in a comforting tone, "we can do a lot quickly with the landscaping. Like, tear it all out. That won't cost any money."

He was right. The scraggly shrubs we had just purchased were easily forty years old, woody and sparse. The house would look better almost immediately with those eyesores gone. I felt myself itching for an axe or a handsaw.

I walked over to the shrubs to gauge how thick their trunks were, and found, upon closer inspection, that ripping them out would be no easy task. They were the Sequoias of shrubs. Removal would have to be done by professionals.

The next day I met with some landscapers who assured me they only needed a couple of hours to wipe the slate clean of shrubs. I gave them the green light. "Take everything out," I said grandly. They promised to return in the morning with the right equipment.

The day passed in a blur of unpacking and organizing, and that evening I went out on the front porch to catch my breath and look one last time upon my weed shrubs. I was walking around them aimlessly when my eye was drawn to an odd-looking space between some branches. I peered more closely at the shrub and found myself eyeball to eyeball with a robin.

She was sitting on a nest, and I was almost certain the nest contained eggs. As we sized each other up she flattened herself down a bit but never moved. She seemed to glare at me with her shiny little eye; she wasn't backing down.

I withdrew first, edging slowly back into the house. As soon as she flew away I dashed out and looked in the nest. Sure enough, four beautiful sky blue eggs were nestled inside of it.

This was a problem. There was absolutely no way we could cut that shrub down now. We had to keep it. My husband sighed but knew me well enough to say nothing. I went to bed and dreamt the landscapers had come earlier than I expected and had cut down the shrub with the nest before I could redirect them. I awoke with the sun and stayed awake; worried the dream would become reality otherwise. I was outside waiting for the landscapers when they arrived.

I explained the situation and instructed them to keep the shrub intact. They did everything but roll their eyes at me. "We will have to charge you extra to come back if you won't let us take this out now," they explained carefully, as if I had some type of auditory disability.

"And, it will look very strange to have only one shrub remaining here. There are plenty of other shrubs. She'll just build another nest somewhere else if this shrub goes."

I held firm. I couldn't explain the look that had passed between me and that mother robin. Her expression said she would die before leaving her eggs. And being a mother myself, I respected that.

The landscapers cleared out every shrub but the nest shrub, and the front of the house looked worse than it had before, which I didn't think was possible. The lone gargantuan unshaped shrub stood in all its glory in our newly cleared front garden, but I didn't care. I felt a kinship with that bird.

As her nest was at my eye level exactly, it allowed me to glimpse her easily. When the eggs hatched I rejoiced. And watched.

When it rained, I watched her puff up and spread her wings over her chicks, reminding me of Ruth 2:12b: "*May you be richly rewarded by the Lord, the God of Israel, under whose wings you have come to take refuge.*" She almost never left, and I assume when she did it was to nourish herself. I never saw any evidence of a male robin, which I surmised was rather unusual. But this mother was stalwart. Even when guys working on the house set up their compressor only feet away from her nest, she just huddled down closer to her babies. The noise from that machine made me jump; I can only imagine how it sounded to her. My pleas to the worker guys to move the compressor fell on deaf ears. The compressor worked there; they would not move it to accommodate a bird.

Weeks passed, the chicks grew and grew, and one day the nest was empty. I was satisfied all was well and eventually the shrub was cut down. But I thought about the bird often.

It was a few months later that a horrifying headline hit the news. A mother was being charged with the death of her young child; she had left her daughter in a hot car while she went in to get a manicure. As a mother of a little girl the same age as the one who died, I was grief stricken.

Oddly enough, it was the image of the bird that added to my grief. A bird, with a brain and reason so much smaller than ours, endured everything for her young. She never left them, not when shrubs around her were being cut down, not when people gazed into her sanctuary, not when compressors belched loudly right outside her shrub. She never left them.

If only humans were more like that bird. If only children were never left, or harmed, or even killed, by their parents. If a bird can get it right, why can't we?

There are probably so many answers, but one has really struck me: the bird isn't tempted to sin. We are. There are so many things that try to lead us away from God in this messy world, and when we succumb to them, there will be consequences — to us, to those we love, or both. Birds don't have to fight the urge to sin. They're birds.

I'm glad God made us as humans; I honestly don't want to be a bird. But I do think we need to slow down to watch and learn from God's creation, because it can teach us so much about humble goodness. A bird was created to care for her chicks; and so are we. The bird does this with a single-minded focus that's beautiful in its simplicity. We, on the other hand, often make our lives harder than they need to be by allowing sin to grab a foothold. When we're tempted, especially by something that may harm our children, we need to remember the robin. We need to hunker down and do what we're called to do, never giving up because we're scared or uncomfortable.

Our front garden has come a long way in the past few years and is now flourishing with young new shrubs and hydrangea bushes. It looks a lot better, I must say. And, to my delight, a robin has chosen one of my new shrubs as her nesting place. Perhaps word got around the bird world that this was a safe house for robins. I hope so.

Barnabas

I cannot imagine life without dogs.

That's why, when my children were four, two and six-months-old, I decided I needed a puppy. My friends said I was crazy. They reminded me I had three little ones and a husband who traveled four days a week. I had a weekly newspaper column, a heavy load of freelance editing work, and a leadership position at my church. It was folly to add another non-toilet trained soul into my household, they insisted. I agreed with everything they said, except the crazy part. In fact, I was certain the crazy thing would be to remain dogless.

I ignored the naysayers and purchased a fuzzy potbellied Golden Retriever baby.

You see, I needed what he could give me: companionship, calmness and adult conversation late at night. And for the past 12 years Barnabas has given me all these things.

Unlike the kids, he was potty-trained in four weeks. And also unlike the kids, he demanded nothing. He just wanted to be with me. And with me he was.

I'm sitting on the hard kitchen floor as I type this, because Barnabas' head is resting on my legs. This is new. He adores me, but he's not a cuddler; he never has been. Lately, however, his habits are changing in a way that makes my heart heavy: He is sleeping often and soundly. Sometimes he doesn't get up until midmorning. He has occasional tremors that distress him. When they start, he immediately finds me and presses against me. I can tell he's scared. That's why I'm sitting on the floor with him now. I'm uncomfortable, but I won't move when my very presence seems to help him feel more secure.

I look down at his familiar face, surprised at the grey that now surrounds his eye sockets and speckles his muzzle. His cheekbones are much more pronounced than they used to be; although he hasn't lost much weight his face has become more sunken. His patient round brown eyes are a bit cloudy. Even his black nose has faded in color.

When I picked him out of the litter he was six weeks old. I'd love to say there was some strategy behind my choice but that's not the case. I'd actually chosen another pup, but he had already been selected. I gazed at the remaining six pups. They all seemed perfect, swarming around me licking and biting. They looked and acted identical. I thrust my hand into the pile of pups and extracted one. The breeder quickly tied a red collar around his neck to mark him, and that was that. He came home when he was ten weeks old.

He was a little fuzz ball with a pointy tail that stood straight up. He cried for his mother the entire first night but never again. Like most Golden Retrievers, he was a breeze to train. Once he understood what I wanted him to do, he'd do it. Simple.

We went to obedience school every week. I really had no time for obedience school and had to pay a babysitter each time we went, but I made it a priority and have never regretted it. It was fun for both of us, but most importantly, it encouraged me to spend one-on-one time with my dog. Between sessions we would work on what we'd learned in class. To this day, he is the most mannerly dog I have ever had.

During those years I would work at night, starting at nine and finishing up about midnight. Before Barnabas, it was lonely. My husband was always out of town and writing late at night has a melancholy feel.

Unless you have a dog with you. Then all is right with the world.

Every night Barnabas would curl up in a tight ball to the left of my desk chair and was with me while I wrote. When I got up to get tea, he would pad into the kitchen and watch me make it. When I sat back down, he would resume his ball. When I read a sentence out loud to him, he'd listen intently.

He came with me to the bus stop every morning and the schoolyard every afternoon. He loved any sort of action: a birthday party, a neighborhood gathering, a cook-out. Like many retrievers, he just enjoyed people and was completely unflappable in large crowds. As social as he was, however, he'd always keep an eye on me. I was his person. And he was my dog.

Thankfully, he still is. Although he's slowed down, I still take him for walks at the park and usually let him off his leash, which will someday earn me a hefty fine, but it will be worth it. As he gallops rather stiffly around the pond he still sports his trademark toothy grin. His enthusiasm is greater than his strength these days and I've been monitoring the walks carefully. A few months ago I took him for a long walk and he seemed sick and shaky that evening. I've been much more careful since then. Even playing ball, his favorite pastime, has been curtailed as of late.

His enthusiasm for tennis balls started at an early age and has only increased with the years. One spring evening when he was two, he came running up to me with a tennis ball and at my request, put it in my hand. I nearly dropped it because it was warm, and damp to boot. I peered at it more closely in the dusk and realized it was a baby bunny. It was wet from Barnabas slobber, but unharmed. Barnabas spun away and returned with another bunny, and another, before I regained my senses and told him to stop. I mopped the babies off, found the nest courtesy of Barnabas, and put them back. I told him not to touch it and he obeyed, gazing yearningly at the nest. The next morning the babies were gone. I think the mother had had enough of strange dogs retrieving her babies and relocated.

Aside from balls and bunnies, Barnabas also takes great joy in retrieving the paper every morning. It is the highlight of his day – it's not a stretch to say we still subscribe to a paper so he can continue his important job. As he trots up the driveway holding the paper, his neck arches and he begins to prance. By the time he enters the house he is strutting proudly and smiling with his eyes, as his mouth is full of paper. Thursdays are good days; on Thursdays we get two papers. The prancing is more pronounced on Thursdays.

I've shifted slightly while writing, trying to get some circulation back into my legs and Barnabas has shifted with me, radiating with uncharacteristic neediness. Things have come full circle.

When I got Barnabas, I needed what he could give me – companionship, security, and a constant love. He gave me all those things and more. Now I feel he's the one seeking these things. His role has shifted from provider to receiver. And that's okay with me.

People often wonder if their dogs will go to heaven. There are many varying opinions but I'm glad that one of my favorite Christian writers, C.S. Lewis, thought it was not only possible, but probable. He writes in *The Problem of Pain,* "….it seems to me that certain animals may have an immortality, not in themselves, but in the immortality of their masters."

My thought is this: Heaven will be perfect. There will be no more pain, or sorrow, or tears.

On top of this biblical promise, we are told that God knows us. Psalm 139:4 tells us, *"Before a word is on my tongue you know it completely, O Lord."* I take great comfort in that fact. Because he knows me, he knows how I feel about my dog. I'm resting in that.

And Barnabas continues to rest on me. I'm going to have to get up soon; I hate to do it but I literally cannot feel my legs any longer. Next time, I'll sit on a cushion.

And I worry about him getting old!

Chapter 4: The Classroom Of Life

Well, I realize that falling down ain't graceful
But I thank the Lord that falling's full of grace
Sometimes I take my eyes off Jesus
And you know that's all it takes
*   —"The Chasing Song", Andrew Peterson*

Working for Wheels

Many women, including some of my closest friends, have a driving need to work full-time outside the home. Sometimes, this need is clearly financial, but sometimes it's not. Sometimes, working seems to revolve around a different kind of need, one I've always supported but never quite understood. Then suddenly, I did. My epiphany began with a phone call a few years ago.

It was the car dealership, announcing our new vehicle was finally in. We could pick it up any time.

I was thrilled. This would be our first brand new vehicle; it was replacing the very staid minivan I'd been driving for eight years. The minivan had stood us well and owed us nothing, but we had purchased it used and there were things about it I would have changed if I could. Our new car was a different story. We choose many different features, including a DVD player and a custom color, an absolutely beautiful deep cobalt blue. The custom color necessitated a seven week delay and I'd been chomping at the bit waiting for it to arrive. Finally, it had come.

Because my husband was out of town, I debated on waiting for him to return before picking up the vehicle. It would be easier, I rationalized, not to get it by myself. After all, we were trading in the van, which meant I had to muck it out and tidy it up. I'd have to drag all three kids into the dealership and listen to their moaning while I dealt with any remaining paperwork and instructions on operating my new car.

But, I decided, we had waited long enough. I was ready to drive my new cobalt blue car and my kids were through the roof about the DVD player. And, I reasoned, wouldn't my husband be surprised when he returned to see the brand new vehicle in our garage? He was busy enough; no, I wouldn't wait for him to pick it up. I'd get it myself and save him the effort. Plus, I'd get the thrill of driving it sooner than later.

I turned my attention to the van. I emptied the glove box and the side compartments. I found one missing boot and two overdue library books. I made sure the van's owner manuals and service records were stacked neatly, and shook out the floor mats. When everything was finally ready, I woke my toddler and rallied the troops.

"We're off to get our new car!" I exclaimed. "We're going to surprise Daddy!" The kids immediately entered into the spirit of the adventure. They climbed into the van and spent the ride to the dealership saying goodbye to it. As we parked it in the dealership lot, I said, dramatically, "That was our last ever ride in our beautiful van. We'll never see her again! Goodbye van!" The kids all chorused their goodbyes, and we trotted happily into the dealership en masse.

My sales guy, Don, pumped my hand enthusiastically, grinning hugely. "It's here, and it's gorgeous. You're going to love this car! Kids, are you ready for your new car?" While he was talking he appeared to be glancing over my shoulder. I finally turned around to see what he was looking at, and seeing nothing, gave him a quizzical look. Seeing my confusion, he blurted out, "Where is your husband?"

"Oh, he's out of town" I replied. Don's face fell. I asked what was wrong and Don looked uncomfortable. "Well, the paperwork is in his name and we need his signatures. We can't release the car to you without him here."

I was stunned. After all, I could sign the papers, couldn't I? I was his wife.

Don scuttled off to speak with his manager, and came back, apologetic. No, that wouldn't work. They could re-do the paperwork, provided, of course, I could verify I had a certain level of income. If I couldn't, we'd all just have to wait until my husband could be on the scene.

I stared at Don. He had, I figured, just started shaving recently, and he was refusing me my vehicle – my income wasn't impressive enough for him. Many scenarios flashed through my mind, including one in which I leaped over Don's desk and grabbed him by his rather fraying tie, but in the end, I gathered my shattered dignity and left without my new car. My son was crying because the surprise for Daddy was ruined and my toddler kept asking to watch Finding Nemo on the new DVD player that we had left on the dealership lot. I seethed the entire way home.

Time is a great cooling agent, and I can now admit something. I did not negotiate for the vehicle myself, even though we were buying it for me. Instead, because of the dislike and disinterest I have for car buying, I designated the duty to my husband. Although he also dreaded the haggling, he cheerfully did it for me. If I had been with him, my name would have also been on the paperwork. So, part of the blame falls squarely in my lap.

But, for the first time, I had a clear understanding of why many women (and men) are reluctant to give up their careers to stay home and raise their children. In our society, our worth remains — in so many ways — linked to our income. It doesn't matter to dealerships and banks that we're bringing up our children to be compassionate, productive members of society. I remember my mother telling me that after she got divorced in the mid-seventies she couldn't get a credit card — despite the fact she had an advanced degree. She had been without an income of her own for a decade; that's what mattered to the bank. And that's why a huge wave of women entered the work force in the seventies and eighties.

They were tired of leaving without their new cars.

Discrimination against women —or anyone for that matter— is wrong. The bible clearly states we're all made in the image of our creator. It also insists we're all equal under Christ Jesus, no matter who we are. *"There is neither Jew nor Greek, slave nor free, male nor female, for you are all one in Christ Jesus"* (Galatians 3:28). My part time writer/full time mom status may not cut it with car dealerships, but I'm confident it's smiled on by the only One who really matters. We're all loved by Him, working or not.

Watching for Dolphins

When I went skydiving in the early nineties, it was thrilling, exhilarating, and probably not the best decision I ever made. After a short one hour training session I found myself in a plane strapped to an instructor I knew nothing about. I just had to trust that he was indeed an expert as billed. As he threw open the plane door and the freezing cold air hit me in the face, I asked myself, quite earnestly, if I was insane. Why was I risking life and limb for this adventure? I didn't like heights. However, in your early twenties you make decisions in context of yourself. Even though I was married during this skydiving adventure, I figured my husband would be okay if my parachute didn't open. Sad, but okay. However, if I had already had children, I never would have gone at all.

That's why, during a recent vacation to Florida, I was mystified to find myself hoisted 600 feet in the air, gazing down at the ocean. I was even more flummoxed to realize two of my children were dangling on either side of me. What had happened here? Why was I taking my life in my hands yet again, and this time, bringing my children along with me? The answer was simple: we were parasailing. From the beach this activity looks harmless, even relaxing. You watch people gently floating in the air, supported by a giant parachute attached to a boat. It really seems like there's nothing to it.

Then you're raised up into the air. When that happens, you realize you're a very, very long way from the water. This did not excite me. But it did excite my children.

Let me backtrack about the children. Parasailing was not what my husband and I had planned for them; we had planned a day of benign, safe digging to China on Clearwater beach, complete with afternoon naps in the pup tent we had purchased for the occasion. But when we hit the beach, the kids pointed excitedly to a parasailer. It did look pretty incredible. The sky was almost cobalt blue without a cloud, the water below was emerald, and the parachutes were bright and enticing. As we watched, the people floating in the air were dropped gently down so their feet touched the water, and then raised back up to new heights. The new sand toys paled in comparison.

The kids begged and pleaded. To squash to revolt we took them to the parasailing booth, certain they were too little to participate. This was the first mistake. The parasailing guys high-fived our kids and asked if they were ready to ride. To my surprised dismay, the height limit for a ride seemed ridiculously low; two of my children towered over the line. We were assured that children (with their parents) were welcome on the parasailing adventure. And so we caved. We left our youngest safely on the beach with her grandparents and fastened life preservers on our thrilled older children.

Minutes later we were on a speedboat with two other guys from Liverpool England. They went first. They were buckled into their harnesses, the harnesses were attached to the parachute, and the boat started accelerating. Instantly, they were lofted into the air. We heard gleeful shouts. "This is bloody amazing! We are lit-rally flying!" They whooped and crowed. I begin to relax. It was obviously an amazing ride.

I asked the boat driver how often he went parasailing. He shot me an incredulous look.

"I never go!" he stated. "I don't do anything that takes my feet off the ground. I think you all have to be crazy, but hey, this job pays the bills. Did I mention we work almost solely for tips?"

I murmured that he had mentioned the tips (this was about the fifth time) and subsided. Before I knew it, harnesses were being strapped on my two children and me. We sat on our bottoms on the boat deck, the boat accelerated, and off we went. Higher. And higher. And higher. We could no longer hear the huge engine on the boat. We could no longer hear anything. We were just floating along in an odd silence. Everything down below seemed sealed off somehow.

The kids were delighted. Swinging their legs, they were turning left and right, taking in the sights. I snapped at them to stay still while I checked the hooks that attached us to the boat. Were they secured tightly? What if one of them broke? Was that really only a rope attaching the three of us to the boat? I had expected a steel cable at the very least. This looked like a waterskiing towline. What if it came untied?

As I worried, my daughter suddenly yelled, "Guys! Look down." I glanced down at the water to see two dolphins swimming right below us. They were jumping and playing; it almost seemed as if they were racing us. It was a beautiful, and thankfully calming, sight.

As we sailed, we saw more dolphins, diving birds, and thankfully, no sharks. I had just started to relax when they began to reel us back into the boat. Our ride was over.

After my husband took his turn, we headed back for shore, exhilarated and dripping wet. The boat crew once again reminded us that they worked for tips. The English guys were jabbering about how great this country was. My husband was asking the boat driver about speeds and elevations. My kids were talking about the dolphins. I just sat in silence.

I was thinking that parasailing really reminded me of life. At times life can be pretty scary indeed. You feel like you're dangling in midair, out of control and adrift. Often you are. But if you look for beauty during those times, you can usually find it. When you do, you can somehow endure the ride. You may not enjoy it, but you can get through it. Whether it's dolphins swimming below you or a tiny hand placed in yours, grace notes help us remember God is ultimately in charge. And that's comforting.

In case you're wondering, we did tip the boat guys, and the boat driver confessed he was fibbing earlier. He loves parasailing, and goes as often as he can.

Very funny.

Peering Past Our Trees

O ne summer our neighborhood lost a lot of trees. "A lot" is a vague word. Let me clarify by giving a rough estimate – well over two dozen. They were all located in a single backyard located diagonally behind mine. I remember the day I noticed all the red twine tied around these trees. My heart sank; surely, these weren't marked for removal? There had to be almost thirty of them; they created their own little forest and were one of the things I loved most about my own yard. I understood the trees were not mine, but somehow even though they were privately owned they seemed to belong to the entire neighborhood. I was grieved, yet my mind supported the rights of property owners to do what they want with their property.

My heart screamed against that right. If I had my way, every tree would stay. Whether a tree is a majestic Black Oak or a small weedy tree, in my mind it's beautiful. Yet, the trees didn't stay. As I feared, every tree that was marked came down. The noise of the destruction was jarring and continued for days, but even more distressing was the ever-widening gaping hole that was now my view from my backyard.

The loss of the trees that summer was hard. My emotions ran the gamut. One day I was furious, another I was weepy. Some days I composed passionate letters to the homeowners that never were mailed. Sometimes I felt, quite frankly, depressed.

After a few weeks of these passions, I pulled myself together and moved on. I had spent enough time I didn't have mourning something I couldn't control. But I couldn't help pondering why my emotions ran so high regarding these felled trees. Why did I object so strenuously to their removal? As the summer rolled on, the answer became clear to me. And it was not an answer I was sure I was comfortable with.

I mourned the loss of the trees because they blocked things. They were beautiful, yes, and green, granted, but first and foremost, they were screens in front of things I'd rather not see or hear. They tempered traffic noise. They blocked garages. They hid garbage cans and compost piles. They surrounded me so much that I rarely pulled my blinds at night.

The trees were so plentiful and dense that I didn't really know what lay beyond them. And I didn't try to find out. I was happy not knowing, secure in my tree-ringed little yard. The trees were more than trees. They were my protectors.

With the loss of my literal trees, I began pondering my figurative ones. What do I keep around me to protect myself from things I don't want to deal with? Several varieties of figurative trees came immediately to mind. Some were growing, while others had become quite stagnant. Some needed to be trimmed back, while others needed to be cut down completely. Still others provided appropriate shading, and needed to remain in my life.

I'm thinking I'm not the only one with a virtual forest of protection around me. Most of us have our own trees in our lives, don't we? These trees may not have trunks and branches and leaves. Instead, they may be an overprotective spouse, or a slanted media outlet, or even a church. Our trees may be a gated community, a certain school, or a certain crowd. If we think about it, we all have trees in our lives that run interference for us. Our trees are different varieties, and some provide larger shade canopies than others, but they all serve the same end.

Partial protection from our trees is not necessarily a bad thing. We do need buffers in our lives. But it's important to recognize the difference between a buffer and a necessity. After all, no tree is forever, as I learned that summer. Even when they seem stalwart and constant, they can be quickly cut down. When they do fall, we don't need to fall with them. Instead, we need to adjust our eyes and hearts to take in and face what is newly revealed to us. Sometimes, we may not like what we see at all. Other times, we may realize the view is not that unpleasant.

Once my literal trees were down, I could see farther and much more clearly than ever before. Some pieces of the view were not what I would have chosen. But I could choose my reaction to these unwanted sights. Other pieces of my now unobstructed view allowed me to see some beautiful things, like the remains of a crumbling stone wall I had never seen before.

I still miss the trees. I miss the beauty they provided and the rustling of their leaves. But the loss of them has taught me to be less hesitant at looking at things head-on. They've also reminded me that the Christian faith focuses not on this daily marred world, but rather a glorious eternal future. There, in heaven, we won't need trees. Our view will be perfect without them.

The Jewels of Life

How often do we stop everything and search for something that is precious to us?

One day I did exactly that. I embarked upon a mission to find a single lost diamond earring. I was certain I would succeed; I just needed to concentrate and retrace my steps. If I stopped running around like a whirling dervish and simply thought about it, I would find it.

The earring was missing, but its mate was not. As I thought about it, I remembered I had taken them off and placed them on top of a bookshelf; now there was only one remaining. The match had to be somewhere in or around the bookshelf.

I started the search by pulling the bookshelf away from the wall (no small feat) and carefully looking and feeling behind it. Aside from some dust balls I found nothing. Undeterred, I then took out every book (again, a huge task), shook it out, paged through it and replaced it. Again, no dice. I pulled back the area rug underneath the bookshelf and found nothing. Well, I thought, maybe I took the earrings out in different places; maybe only looking around the bookshelf was self-defeating. I expanded my search to the entire house, looking under every piece of furniture, in every drawer and under every rug. I checked my daughter's Barbie box to make sure the earring hadn't found its way into a Barbie ear, and looked through my eight-year-old's treasure box. I checked bathrooms, windowsills and the laundry area. The more I searched the more determined I became. I could find this. I lost it; I could find it. I just had to try harder.

I finally took a Diet Coke break and called a friend. After listening to my plight, she suggested I search my vacuum cleaner bag. At first I dismissed the idea. No way was I sifting through the contents of a vacuum bag to find a tiny earring. But then I remembered I was a mother, who, until only recently, had two kids in diapers. I also had a large dog. The messes I had tackled in the past seven years were legendary. Who was I to be delicate?

I brought the vacuum bag outside and went to work. The contents weren't nearly as bad as I had feared – just a lot of dust. Encouraged, I sifted through this gray silt, depending on my sense of touch to find and pull things out of the dust. To my delight, I found the earring back, and then the earring setting. Surely, the diamond was here, it would just take patience to pull it out. I searched and sifted for a long time, but could not find the diamond.

I was completely baffled. The other pieces were there; where was the prize piece? I sifted through the dust patiently, again and again. I found nothing more than the wishbone piece from my daughter's Operation game.

The sun began to set, making my expedition that much harder. I finally straightened up and admitted defeat. The diamond was lost. Despite my resolve and careful efforts, I hadn't found it.

I slowly started cleaning up the mess. Oddly, I did not consider those hours searching for the diamond wasted. Instead, I felt they had reminded me of something I seldom pause to consider.

God has given me many, many precious things. And for the most part, I don't take the time to really concentrate on them until they're gone. Like the diamond, they're almost impossible to repossess, no matter how hard I try.

I'm thinking many of us struggle with this reality. As I searched for my tiny diamond, I realized afresh how much my earrings meant to me. They were a Christmas gift from my husband, and my heart leaped when he placed the little red box in my hands. When I opened the lid and saw the glistening studs, I burst into tears. Except for my engagement ring, they were the first diamonds I'd ever received. But earrings, after all, are replaceable. Many things are not.

People are the real jewels in this life. People like childhood friends, grandparents and parents. People like your children. There are so many times I wish for another day with my grandmother, for example. I wish I had taken the time to answer every letter she so faithfully wrote to me. But I didn't. In my 20-year-old reality, I was just too busy, and now she's gone. I want to write back. But I can't.

People are the diamonds of life, but there are also many rubies and emeralds mixed in. We need to remember to appreciate those more modest gems as well: our dogs, the smell of our houses, our hydrangea bushes, and the nest of birds behind the shutter. We need to give thanks for our neighbors, our teachers and our pastors. We need to revel in those things that make our lives a bit more sparkly.

Don't wait to pick through the dust for your treasures, as I did. You may indeed be luckier than I; you may find yours that way. But the search is messy and tiresome, and most importantly, it can be avoided. Give thanks for the jewels of life *before* they're lost.

I never did find my diamond. But I gained something even more valuable: a reminder that I've been given many riches in this life. I should enjoy them while I've got them.

Chapter 5: Home Is Where The Heart Is

Be grateful for the home you have, knowing that at this moment, all you have is all you need.
—Sarah Ban Breathnach

There's no Place like Home

Wrapping my hands around my coffee cup to combat the early morning chill, I gazed at the Rocky Mountains and lamented that we lived in the Midwest. My usual morning coffee scenery is not so inspiring; if I'm lucky, I might see a squirrel or two while sitting on my porch. This Colorado view was majestic and at the same time soothing. As I drank it in, I mentally scolded myself for voluntarily remaining in my hometown. Where was my sense of adventure? America is a huge country, and for most of our lives my husband and I have only lived in a tiny part of it. We hadn't planned to remain in the town in which we both grew up; when we were first married, we were ready to move anywhere. Yet somehow, we remained stuck in Wheaton like moss on a log.

My parents had the right idea, I thought. They had left congestion and high property taxes behind and moved to 35 mountain acres outside of a tiny town in Colorado. You could not hear any traffic.

You could not hear anything but birds and the rustling of the grasses. You could not see other houses, garages, or streetlights. Every direction you looked, you could see only mountains. What an incredible way to live!

I spent several hours on the porch dreaming about relocating. It would be easy, I thought. All we needed to do was find my husband a new job, sell our house, buy a new one, find new schools, make new friends, and start over in every way. It was possible.

I finally shook myself into reality and realized we had to get some supplies. We needed certain kid foods, I had forgotten a sweatshirt for my son, and I wanted to get some really nice steaks for dinner. I asked my parents how to get to the nearest town, stressing I required a good grocery store.

They creased their brows. The town was about 15 minutes away down the dirt roads, they said, but you won't find everything you need there. There was only a tiny grocery store and a pharmacy. You'd better drive out to Walmart.

I explained again I needed steaks, and maybe some asparagus. They nodded. You can get those at Walmart, they assured me. When you live out here, you get everything at Walmart. There's no other place to go.

I relented and asked how far away it was. Not far, was the reply. Only about thirty-five minutes.

Thirty-five minutes.

I made the trek, and did indeed find everything on my list. However, the jaunt took up the better part of my morning.

Later that day, just as dusk was beginning to creep over the mountains, I once again surrendered to a sense of well-being. From the house, I watched the kids and dogs romping around in the clearing. What a place! Our kids loved running around the property. As far as I was concerned, they could play outside until they dropped.

But not as far as my parents were concerned. A few minutes later, they were calling the kids and dogs in from the yard. I protested. Why not let them stay outside? They were having so much fun.

Well, because they shouldn't be outside after a certain time of day, they replied. We don't even keep the dogs out when it gets dark, because of the bears and the mountain lions. We've seen tracks; they're out there. So it's best the kids be inside at dusk.

Bears and mountain lions.

The next night, my parents invited the neighbors, Mr. and Mrs. Ex, over to meet us. These neighbors lived a few miles down the dirt road, and as they were about our age and had kids, my parents thought we'd hit it off.

And we did. We grilled, relaxed, and chatted. The kids played nicely together. All was going well until my husband mentioned he had seen a rattlesnake on the dirt road. Mrs. Ex perked up immediately. "What did you do with it?" she asked eagerly. My husband looked perplexed. "Nothing," he admitted. "I didn't get too close to it."

"Too bad!" she lamented. "They make great eating. Whenever I see one, I kill it and put it on the grill!"

I stopped chewing my hamburger.

Mrs. Ex continued her snake recipe, unheeding of our mounting horror. "First, I grab a pitchfork and pull it out straight. Then, I take a shovel and chop off its head." At this point she paused in her narrative to give a remarkable physical demonstration of the head chopping technique. "Then, I marinate it in garlic and herbs and throw it on the grill. Makes a wonderful appetizer."

Grilled rattlesnake.

I remain in awe of the Eden-like landscape of Colorado; our God is certainly one of beauty. I still wish I could drink my coffee each morning while staring at the mountains. But maybe, just maybe, my Chicago suburb isn't so bad.

I'm finding myself appreciating the beauty of lush, green, flat land. I'm enjoying the quick jaunt to purchase almost anything. I love that my kids can walk in our yard at night without bumping into anything more than a cicada. And I'm especially enjoying my neighbors, who do grill, but only packaged meats.

There's no place like home.

The Farmette

For years, my husband and I had been craving space. Not necessarily a larger house, but more land. Since our mid-twenties, we'd yearned for some acres to call our own; a place with woods, water and serenity. We wanted a weekend home, a place to spread our wings and focus on what was truly important. The suburbs were wearing on us and while we didn't see the logic of moving to the country full-time we wanted someplace to escape to and perhaps live full-time down the road. We weren't exactly sure what we wanted in a retreat property. But we were quite sure about what we didn't want.

We didn't want this paradise to be more than a few hours away. We didn't want to be by a busy road of any kind, we didn't want less than five acres, and we didn't want to spend a lot of money. These requirements pointed us to many properties labeled by the same name: farmettes.

Farmettes are usually billed as old and charming original farmhouses with wooded acres and a stream. In fact, the descriptions included in these farmette listings conjure up images of playing Scrabble by the fire, taking long relaxed walks in the country, and simply spending quality time with your family. Fall leaves would be more vibrant there, snowfalls more magical, stars more brilliant.

We were all too aware that many of these vintage houses would need some work. However, somehow my husband and I had been lulled into believing that working on the farmette would be part of its allure. Whether we were painting fences or upgrading knob and tube wiring, we would be together, creating a country retreat for our family and friends. Not surprisingly, the fact that we barely had time to do laundry at home didn't figure into these dreams. If we had the vacation home, we thought, somehow extra time would come.

Our images of the quality of life provided to us by these farmettes were much more attractive than the farmettes themselves. We had traveled to view several and come away discouraged. One didn't have working plumbing, another was by a busy granite quarry, yet another had a four lane highway running behind it. But we're optimists by nature. Surely, we told ourselves, something would pop up. In the meantime, we were conducting a slow and somewhat painful search for our weekend retreat.

Suddenly, it seemed like I had found it. I had discovered it in a rural real estate publication and contacted the listing agent. A very friendly man, he told me it was secluded and was not near any major highways. In fact, he insisted, I would love the location of this property. He sounded a bit puzzled when he assured me that yes, there was working plumbing and no, there was no quarry nearby, but I had learned to be thorough before embarking upon long treks to view farmettes.

I was more excited than I cared to admit. Granted, I'd been let down before when searching for vacation property, but this one seemed like a dream come true. It was only two hours away; it had a winding stream, acreage, and a lovely old farmhouse with a generous front porch. The price was also right. I decided to call an impromptu road trip and asked several girlfriends to go with me to see it. We could walk the property together, inspect the house, and then have a leisurely lunch while brainstorming decorating ideas for the old farmhouse.

My girlfriends became infected by my farmette fever and jumped on the road trip idea with enthusiasm. (This was probably due to the incentive of going anywhere without children; the husbands would take over for the afternoon). Perhaps, they suggested, it could be a mini retreat for sorority reunion gatherings. They also agreed, squinting at the grainy black and white photo of the house, that it could become a majestic generational home. In fact, they would enjoy saying they were with me the first time I viewed it.

We exited the interstate according to the agent's directions and found ourselves in a bustling little town. "It doesn't look very remote," observed one of my friends. I assured her that the farmette itself was on a small rural road; we were just getting to that gravel path. I advised patience as we stopped for a red light and glanced at the directions again. "It says turn left here," a girlfriend instructed. "But after that, there are no more directions. Is there another page?"

I grabbed the directions from her and looked at the road sign for this busy four-way intersection. The road sign said Hattay Drive. The house address said Hattay Drive. My remote farmette was located on this busy thoroughfare. No, it was not a highway; the agent had been right about that. But it was not a remote gravel road by any stretch.

The car became quiet. We turned left and found the farmette located in the middle of two cornfields. Incredibly huge power lines and towers loomed on either side of the house. Cars and trucks whizzed by on the road. The house looked much better in the grainy photograph than it did in real life. The winding stream was nowhere in sight.

We turned the car around and got back on the interstate. Silence reigned for the first few miles. One of my friends attempted conversation. "So that was a farm-lette," she mused. "Very interesting."

I reminded her it was called a farmette, not a farmlette. Other than that, I didn't have anything else to say.

We'd keep dreaming. And we'd keep trying. We knew it was out there somewhere.

Dream Homes

T here's nothing like the house you grew up in. You remember its smell, the flecks in the linoleum on the kitchen floor, and the handles on the cabinets. You could place every piece of furniture in its original spot in the living room, and you could pinpoint the permanent stain caused by the dog getting sick on fondue oil. You remember it all, although you haven't seen it for years, perhaps decades. If you could go back and look at it again, you would.

That's what someone did with her childhood house, which just happened to now be mine. One day a car drove slowly toward my house and stopped, engine idling. A woman was staring at my house. I mean, really staring. Although I thought my house was cute, it was not one that people usually stopped to admire. My curiosity was sparked.

As I walked up to the car, the woman seemed somewhat flustered. "Is this your house?" she asked. "My name's Paula. I grew up in this house, and just wanted to show my kids the front of it. I have many great memories of this house."

I knew at once that I should ask her in. After all, I would love to be re-introduced to my childhood home. But then I remembered not a single bed was made. The egg pan was still on the stove, and laundry piles were sitting on the kitchen counters. I hesitated, and she picked up on that immediately. "I just wanted to drive by," she re-iterated. I took a steadying breath, thought about what the bible said about hospitality, and insisted she come in. I found — to my surprise — that I really wanted her to.

She was out of the car like a shot. She gave an involuntary sigh of contentment as she stepped over the threshold. I understood her sentiments exactly.

To this day, I remember not only the inside but also the outside of my childhood home. I remember the wallpaper in my parent's bedroom, the smell of the basement, and the number of stairs to the second floor. I can identify every tree and shrub that grew in and around our yard; some I avoid to this day, others I plant because I loved them then and want them now. These details are permanently etched in my brain, even though I moved from that house when I was twelve. In different cycles of my life, I dream about that house. In these dreams, I'm living my present life, with my husband and children, in my childhood home. It's as though I've never left it.

Despite the laundry piles and the egg pan (or perhaps, because of them) Paula too, seemed to feel as if she had never left. She reminisced about secret hiding places she and her sisters used to curl into. She checked the tops of the banisters to see if they still came off. When she was little she hid many treasures inside those banisters. She told me where the basement stairs used to be, enlightened me on the name of our kitchen cabinet maker, and told me the story behind the beam in our kitchen. This enormous, solid oak beam on our kitchen ceiling has puzzled many a contractor. Paula told me it was a railroad tie on the old railroad track that is now the Illinois Prairie Path. She remembers her mother, vastly pregnant at the time, helping her father manipulate the beam into the kitchen. Not, we both agreed, the most sensible endeavor, but all ended well.

After thanking me profusely for the tour, Paula left. As I watched her drive away I pondered the true meaning of home. A real home is a refuge, a comfort, and a place where one feels secure and loved. That's why, I believe, our childhood homes remain alive in our memories. We don't yearn for them because they were showplaces or picture perfect. We're nostalgic for them because we were (at least most of us) loved in them. That was what made our homes beautiful.

As we grew older, we were told things other than love made a house beautiful. We became victims of the Martha Stewart era, where homes had to be large, perfectly decorated, and bursting with vases of freshly cut flowers from our own garden. We've been trained to believe that without these ingredients our homes just won't cut it.

I cannot recall a vase of freshly cut flowers ever gracing the house I grew up in, yet that house is —literally — the house of my dreams. We need to remember that love is what makes our houses homes. Perhaps that's the power of our childhood homes; children respond to love, not perfect decorating or impressive square footage. When you're surrounded by love in a place, you naturally remember that place and yearn to return to it. That's why our childhood homes are often our dream homes.

I'm so glad Paula stopped by to revisit the place where she felt loved and secure. It's encouraged me to do the same; I'm going to knock on the door of my childhood home and see if an invitation to enter is forthcoming. I hope it is, but if it's not, I'll just sneak in a quick sniff of the front entry. It will be enough.

The Mudroom

For years, I had been yearning for a mudroom. A really big, gleaming, well organized mudroom. One bursting with cubbies, adorned with hooks, and lined with bead board. A room that could easily accommodate three children, their parents, and an overexcited Golden Retriever. If I had that mudroom, I figured, all my problems would miraculously diminish.

Of course, I already had a mudroom. My mudroom was a four-by-four foot square of peel and stick tile. When we walked in the back door, coated with mud or snow, all five of us carefully squeezed onto the square and bent down to remove our shoes. While we were attempting this, the dog often leapt over our heads to exit the back door. The entire operation became trickier because the tiled square was located at the top of the basement stairs. Luckily, the stairs were carpeted.

I'd been wracking my brain for a solution to my mudroom dilemma. Sure, there were worse problems. But certainly, something could be done to alleviate this one. So I talked with my husband about breaking out the mudroom and making a bigger one. It would be a breeze, I argued. After all, it's only a square room.

My husband had a different opinion. He pointed out ground would have to be broken, a new foundation poured, and the operation would disrupt our lives for months. Why not, he suggested reasonably, think about pushing out the entire back of the house if we're going to undertake a project? That way, we'll have a bigger kitchen with a better work pattern.

We both agreed that was the wiser route to consider. After all, if we were going to remove walls, why not get a better kitchen at the same time? We didn't even have a dishwasher in our current kitchen; updates were certainly in order. And, new energy efficient appliances would make financial sense down the road. We owed it to ourselves and the environment to upgrade. The decision made, we called a few builders and set up some meetings.

Before our first meeting, a friend asked us what renovations we were considering. When we told him, he furrowed his brow. "Are you building over the new kitchen?" he asked. We replied that no, we were not. "Well you should! Throw a bigger bedroom over the top of it as long as you're pouring a foundation. If you pour a foundation and don't build a two-story addition, you're wasting money."

My husband and I were overwhelmed at the brilliance of this logic. Of course, we'd build a big master bedroom over the kitchen addition. After all, it would be economical in the long run, and would add a lot of value to our house as well.

We met with the first builder and told him our plans. He agreed we were thinking ahead by building a second story, and asked if he could make another suggestion. Why not, he said wisely, dig a new basement underneath this addition? That way, we could get three stories out of the construction. And, it would be virtually impossible to add a full basement later.

We agreed with feeling. Of course, we should add a basement, preferably one with nine- foot ceilings. We could use it for so many things. It could be an exercise room, a guest room, an office, or all three. The possibilities were endless. It would only make sense to dig the basement when we did the other renovations.

We met with several other builders and sat back happily to await their estimates. As additions go, we told ourselves, ours was relatively modest. It was just tall.

I started to dreamily peruse magazines showcasing incredible kitchens, perfect for a family of five with a dog. I leafed through catalogs for a bedroom set for our new master bedroom. I picked out paint colors and hooks for the wall of the now overshadowed new mudroom. It was a time of supreme well-being and contentment.

Then the bids came in.

After we stopped gasping like beached fish, my husband and I regrouped. Did we really need the basement? The master bathroom? The larger kitchen? What were we willing to cut out? What did we really need?

(The timing of this soul-searching exercise was providential. For some time, we'd been grappling with stewardship and what exactly it should look like for us. After all, everything we have is from God.

How much, then, should we be giving back to Him, and what do we feel right about keeping?)

The answer to the "what do we need" question was sobering. We only needed a bigger entryway, and need was a strong word for even that. We just didn't feel we could justify spending such a large amount of money on extra room that would be luxurious, but not necessary. The bids were filed away for posterity, and we began the long journey of working with our existing space to make it more efficient. The mudroom would remain as it was; the kitchen and bathrooms would get updated. No walls would be moved.

But oh, it was a thrill to imagine, plan and design what could have been. I enjoyed the thought of our pricy addition almost as much as the real thing. Perhaps I even enjoyed the vision more than the actuality. After all, dreaming is free.

Dreaming allows for the utopia life often does not.

The Missing Piece vs. Missing the Peace

I was thrilled to see the large white truck back into my driveway. Finally, one of the last pieces of my new kitchen had arrived. For weeks I had been awaiting my island countertop. It was the missing piece of a very complex kitchen construction puzzle; everything else was in place. With the installation of this long-awaited island top, I'd finally have a complete working kitchen.

Until I saw the truck, I didn't really believe I'd ever see a countertop on my island. In fact, I was getting pretty used to the piece of plywood that was serving as our surface. But now the counter people were here, carefully unloading a large wrapped parcel from the truck. The two guys who had been working on my kitchen for months were also present, and seemed almost as excited as I was. They quickly rearranged their tools and made space for the counter to be set down on the island.

I led the counter guys to the kitchen, and watched with bated breath as they hoisted the huge piece of countertop onto the top of the island. They quickly removed the wrapping and whipped out their tools to fasten it down. I did not want to believe what I was seeing, and for a beat of time debated on ignoring what I knew to be true. Common sense quickly prevailed and I asked the guys to take the top away. They stared at me.

"Why? It's cut perfectly," they insisted.

"It's the wrong color," I muttered.

They laughed and kept adjusting the top. I realized they thought I was kidding. I spoke a little louder. "Guys! This is not my countertop! It's the wrong color! This is not the color I chose." In case they still didn't believe me, I showed them my sample. It was a very deep red. The counter was a bright cherry red. Silence descended over the room. Everyone looked at everyone else.

Almost simultaneously, the cell phones were whipped out. My kitchen guys called their bosses. The counter guys called their bosses. It was quickly determined how the mistake was made, and also quickly determined there was nothing anyone could do about it. The counter would have to be remade; the new top would be ready in about four weeks. The counter guys bid us a sunny farewell, removed the offending piece, and left.

For about five minutes I had a countertop.

My head started a dull throbbing. I took two Excedrin and went up to my desk, feeling extraordinarily sorry for myself. Now I would be waiting for weeks and weeks for the missing piece. Why had this happened?

The ringing phone snapped me out of my misery. Grabbing it, I was greeted by the voice of a good friend, who noticed immediately I seemed down. I relayed my tale of woe and she made the appropriate sympathetic noises. Then she mentioned a friend's husband had just come home from a mission trip to Bolivia.

She talked about the sights he had seen and the lives he had touched. Because this missionary man is a doctor, his main purpose for the trip was to treat burn victims. Since many people still cook in a single pot over an open fire, he had plenty of business.

Their quality of life is unbelievably different than ours. Every chore is done manually, with great time and effort. Where this doctor was visiting, life is not easy. Luxuries are few, and hardships are many. But that was not what made an impression on this missionary. What really impacted him was not what these people didn't have, but what they do have.

They have happiness. They're not always searching for more; they're living for the moment, and full of joy. I can't stop thinking about these folks in Bolivia. They are content living in conditions that would make us scream.

And I wanted to scream over a countertop.

This phone call reminded me again of something I know, but often forget. God has given me so much — my blessings are too numerous to count. Yet somehow, I manage to take them for granted. I instead ruminate about what I don't have.

It seems, as a society, the more we get, the more we want. We have a driving thirst for more of everything. Even as we drink, we are desperate for a taller glass of colder water. We become convinced that our thirst can only be quenched by acquisition.

Contentment and peace do not come from our external circumstances, but rather Christ within us. External things can bring us temporary happiness, certainly, but as we know, external things can be broken, or lost, or the wrong color. These folks in Bolivia may have been poor in material things, but they were rich in spirit, because they focused on the only thing that never breaks, is always perfect, and never changes. They were spirit-filled Christians, living for their faith and faith alone.

The correct countertop did eventually arrive, and another family is now enjoying it, because we moved not long after our kitchen was finally completed. The countertop is no longer in my life, but Christ still is, of course. Unlike anything external, He'll be with me wherever I go, including Heaven. I'm betting there are not many countertops there. Just a thought.

Chapter 6: Glittering Holiday Treasures

It is good to be children sometimes, and never better than at Christmas when its mighty Founder was a child Himself.
— Charles Dickens

Resurrecting Our Joy

When we were kids, Easter egg hunts were incredibly exciting. They were also serious business.

You focused on being fast, and having an eagle eye. You glanced everywhere, shrieking in delight when you spied a glimpse of color. As you grabbed each egg, you were already seeking the next one. There was no time to savor your acquisition; rather, each discovery whetted your appetite for more. You ran around like a dervish until the adults told you all the eggs had been found. Even then, while counting your loot, you furtively glanced around the yard in hopes of spying an overlooked egg. Sometimes it happened, and an immediate fight amongst the kids would ensue. As the egg hunt had been officially suspended, the kids who didn't find the stray egg would insist the finder did not merit the treasures inside. They must be split evenly (almost impossible) or returned to an adult.

These memories were racing through my mind during our neighborhood Easter egg hunt. Two adjoining yards were transformed into virtual treasure troves of filled plastic eggs. Eggs were balanced in tree branches, stuck behind porch lights, perched on fence posts, and stuffed in gutters. Everywhere you looked there was a splash of color. It was a sight to behold.

The actual egg hunt was too. As the dozens of children poured over the two yards, the adults watched with unconcealed glee. The younger children toddled purposely toward specific eggs, stepping over numerous unnoticed eggs on the way to their destination. Kindergarteners ran around as quickly as they could, yelling and laughing with each found treasure. They would occasionally point an over-stimulated toddler toward an obvious egg. The older kids prided themselves on finding the more difficult eggs, climbing on play sets and trees to dislodge them. Some kids had scouted the perimeter before the hunt began, and raced deliberately toward the biggest eggs. The two yards looked like an anthill, with kids swarming over every nook and cranny.

When the eggs were all gathered, phase two of the outing began. Some children hunkered down and started opening their treasures. Others carefully counted their eggs and gave some away to those who weren't as lucky. (This was a relative judgment, as every child gathered more eggs than they could shake a stick at). Some didn't touch their loot, but gave their baskets to their parents for safekeeping.

One toddler sat down on a concrete slab, opened his eggs, and steadily ate jelly bean after jelly bean.

The anticipated shout of joy came from a third grade boy who didn't quite believe the adults' assurances that all the eggs were found and had discovered a straggler nestled in a dormant clematis vine. He held it up triumphantly only to have his dad appropriate it so peace would be kept. Nothing ever seems to change.

Some people I know become rather impatient with egg hunts. After all, they insist, Easter is not about eggs and candy. It's about something far more important. And of course, they're right.

Easter is about the resurrection of Jesus — the axis of Christianity. No Easter, no Christians. Obviously, I agree that the Easter Bunny shouldn't get top billing. He is not the star of this holiday.

But I think the egg hunts during Easter are marvelous, because they generate an excitement in young children that unadorned theology often cannot. This excitement can provide the perfect springboard for talking to our kids about the real sweetness of Easter – the Resurrection. And, I might add, Jesus himself was very inclusive and complimentary to children and their simple faith. In fact, He insisted, they were the ones who really understood what was important. Their little hearts were ready to receive Him, while the mature, scholarly hearts of many were not.

Hearts often do become a bit tougher, a bit more cynical, with age. That hasn't changed since the days Jesus walked the earth. Sometimes we forget the simple joys of love, faith, and surprises. Children do not. The enthusiasm they show during a simple egg hunt reminds us of that. While we watch them, our hearts become a bit more flexible again. We remember the thrill of the hunt, the anticipation of the unknown, and the security of knowing our parents were overseeing and loving us. We remember the excitement – and the childlike joy – of Easter.

Perhaps if we recapture the excitement, we can also become impervious to the cold, as our children seemed to be that weekend. As the parents shivered, blew on their hands and drank hot coffee, the kids raced around with unzipped coats and begged to take them off. They were utterly comfortable that frigid afternoon, while most of the parents were miserably chilled.

Come to think of it, I never remember being cold during a childhood Easter egg hunt either. Joy must be a warming agent.

Skeletons and Spiders

I awoke to moist breathing in my left ear. As my husband was already at work, I narrowed down the breather to either my Golden Retriever or a child. I gingerly cracked my eyes and found myself staring directly at my son. Our noses were almost touching.

"Mom, can I please have the spider web stuff. Please? It's almost Halloween. I really want to put it outside. If I don't put it up soon, Halloween will be over and I'll have to wait until I'm in second grade. That's a long time. Seriously."

I rolled over to my other side and looked at the clock. 6:05 a.m. I reached for the remote and turned on the television to confirm what I thought was the date. When CNN assured me I wasn't crazy, it was indeed only September 25th, I turned back to face my son. In what I hoped was a convincing, authoritative tone, I told him Halloween was over a month away. I assured him if we put our decorations out too early, they would be destroyed by squirrels and rain by Halloween. I also stressed that if we started celebrating Halloween before mid-October, he would be tired of Halloween before it began. My voice dwindled away as I realized it was over; there was no way I could resist his earnest face.

In my defense, I had resisted his little boy cuteness for more than two weeks – this was not a new early morning discussion. My arguments were wearing thin. So was my resolve.

"Please!" he begged, opening his eyes even wider so they looked like big round chestnuts. "I've been waiting for a really long time." I had to admit, in his understanding of time, he had.

I briefly debated holding out a few more weeks, but even entertaining the thought made me weary. Maybe if I relented I would be able to sleep until 6:30 or so, just once. "Okay," I muttered.

My son shrieked with unadulterated joy and flew downstairs. I heard him opening the front hall closet and rooting around in the crackling plastic bag that held our Halloween decorations. The front door slammed and he was off.

A half hour later I crept downstairs and took an apprehensive look at my front garden. My huge Black-Eyed Susans were unrecognizable. They were coated with sticky white webbing studded with plastic spiders. This webbing stuff, when stretched out with care, can actually make one think some huge mutant spider happened along and spun a pure white crystallized creation. But when it's distributed in large clumps, it doesn't resemble much of anything. My flowers did not look as though they were covered in webbing, but rather beaten down by a large snowfall.

I asked my son if he wanted help stretching out the webbing. He looked at me with pity. "No thanks Mom. This is exactly how I want it."

I was afraid of that.

A bit later I heard him pulling a chair around in the basement. My ears perked up immediately, as any parent's would. The sound of a chair being pulled means a child is trying to grab something that has been placed deliberately out of reach. A few minutes later my son came up the stairs beaming triumphantly. He had in his hand a talking skeleton.

This full size skeleton hung on your front door and greeted trick-or-treaters as they approached your house. He was pre-programmed with four different pithy comments, and was funny for about two minutes. Then he became old. Why we owned it I didn't know, but I was betting my husband had something to do with its purchase.

I took one look at my son's excited face and sadly went to the front door to take down the new harvest berry wreath I had hung a few days earlier. I now had a grotesque skeleton and lumps of white cotton showcasing my house. Talk about curb appeal!

However, I wasn't helping myself. Just one day earlier, I had caved and sprang for two huge hairy spiders at Target. I didn't want them any more than I wanted bones hanging on my front door, but somehow I had walked out with them. In my defense, though, my son discovered and asked for many more things on that shopping expedition. They included, but were not limited to: pumpkin place mats, bat napkin rings, hanging witches, steaming cauldrons, hairy spiders that hang from strings, dog Halloween costumes, bats that fly, plastic jack-olanterns that talk, pumpkin pencils and treat buckets. That we got out of there at all still amazes me.

C.S. Lewis once wrote that he was surprised by joy. This is an all too common adult affliction — kids are usually a different story. One of the things I adore about my son is his effusive joy. He simply bursts with it. And, I would have been the first to admit, even without clumpy spiderwebs adorning my front garden, my house was hardly a showplace. It was however, a home, my son's as much as any of ours. And a home should give joy.

I just wished my son found joy in mums and berry wreaths.

Thanking Our Soldiers

The wind seemed to be getting colder by the minute. As it bit my cheeks and stung my eyes, I clutched my three–year-old a bit closer to me. She let out a squall of protest, lamenting, "I can't see Grandpa when you squeeze me! Stop squeezing!"

I relaxed my grip slightly, and my daughter readjusted herself so she could see the flagpole with the veterans sitting proudly underneath it. One of those veterans was my stepfather, her grandpa. And he was, for the first time in many years, being honored on Veteran's Day.

That year our public schools were open on Veteran's Day for the first time in my recollection. At first, I was shocked and not altogether happy about that decision. Why couldn't the kids have Veteran's Day off like they always had? After all, it was an extremely important day. It should be marked, I thought, and lamented the district's decision to keep the schools open.

No doubt my fondness of Veteran's Day can be, in part, directly related to my family veteran count: my small family boasts five military veterans. Two were active duty until very recently, and had served in Iraq and Afghanistan for several years. But I believe my passion about Veteran's Day runs deeper than my family history. In my mind, we owe our veterans our very existence. They've promoted democracy throughout the world, while keeping our shores safe at home. They are the ones who have experienced the horrors of war, asking for nothing but gratitude and support from their country.

Serving in the military is not an easy path, but for many reasons, men and women proudly choose it. Unless they obtain a high rank there is little glory. There is also little pay. But there is honor. And friendships. And the knowledge that some how, some way, they're making the world a better place to live. Veterans deserve our admiration and gratitude.

That's why I was initially so fussed that first year our schools remained open on Veteran's Day. How would the children understand and honor our veterans?

I was delighted to admit my reservations were misplaced. The kids honored and celebrated our veterans because the schools were in session. Instead of sleeping late and watching TV during the day, our children participated in a Veteran's Day ceremony at our elementary school. The red carpet was rolled out for veterans in what was the first of many Veteran's Day ceremonies to come.

The principal pulled out all the stops during this groundbreaking event. The students sat solemnly in their lines while a moment of silence was instituted for the soldiers who gave the ultimate sacrifice for their country. Fifth graders then read touching stories about veterans and their dedication. A Girl Scout troop solemnly raised the American flag. The principal gave a short — but heart-felt — tribute to the veterans.

Most importantly, the veterans who were attending the ceremony were all thanked – individually— and handed a rose. Some were young, some were old. Some leaned heavily on canes; another was in a wheelchair. Each approached the podium proudly when his or her name was called, and each received thunderous applause from hundreds of students and parents.

That's the way it should be.

After reciting the Pledge of Allegiance and singing God Bless America, a single trumpeter played Taps, signaling the event's end. All in all, the program had lasted for about a half hour.

Later, I asked my stepfather, a World War II veteran, what he thought of the ceremony. I expected a polite, but somewhat disinterested, answer. To my surprise his eyes welled up with tears. He simply shook his head.

"Didn't you like it?" I asked nervously. He nodded and choked through his tears, "I loved it. It was the best Veteran's Day I can remember."

I found out later our school's tribute was one of the very few Veteran's Day celebrations he had ever been invited to. I doubt he was alone. It seems Veteran's Day has so often been about a day off from school and store sales, instead of honoring those for which it was instituted. I'm sure my stepfather's sentiment was shared by many of the 30 or so veterans who also participated in this unique ceremony.

For the first time, many school children understood who veterans really were. They were their grandpas, their fathers, and their uncles. They were their aunts and older brothers. They were real, and they were honored.

It seems so little to offer these men and women who have given us so much. But, judging my stepfather's response to his rose and the applause, it may be all they really want.

There's much we can't do for our soldiers. We can't erase bad memories or heal old wounds. But we can – and should – be praying for them, with gratitude and thankful hearts.

Praying with the Pilgrims

S everal years ago we traveled through the Netherlands and explored a town called Leiden. It was to Leiden that the Pilgrims fled and settled before they sailed for America in 1620. Intrigued by that fact, we found and walked through the home site where our founders lived almost 400 years ago. It was thrilling to think we were touching the very stone walls they had touched, and walking through the courtyard they had walked. This monument is and was in the very heart of a beautiful, cultured city, so it's amazing to remember what welcomed the Pilgrims in our land.

They were greeted by sheer wilderness, strange terrain and even stranger food choices. Life was, in their new and free land, a struggle — often a fatal one. Yet even in the midst of all their hardships, the pilgrims gave thanks. They sat down and broke bread together, thanking God for all the blessings they'd received. So Thanksgiving was born.

Until our visit to Leiden, I had never really pondered Thanksgiving. I'd enjoy the day, and display the dozens of turkey-inspired crafts my children brought home from school. I would revel in the long weekend and the relaxed schedule, but seldom did I think of the vital lessons of the first Thanksgiving.

Thanksgiving is chock-full of meaning, but you have to turn it over and over in your mind for the beauty to shine through. In fact, many things in our lives fall into this category – we're surrounded by beautiful, common things and events that we often take for granted. Mallard ducks are the perfect example of this – that God created them is indeed compelling evidence for a loving creator God. But like so many things, Mallard ducks are not usually appreciated.

After all, these ducks are everywhere. Even though we've seen them thousands of times, we don't really watch as a shaft of sunlight transforms the male's green head into a myriad of colors. Each feather glistens with aqua, forest green and kelly green highlights. The white feathers on their bodies are all edged with brown or black and fit together in an inconceivable web of function. These feathers are created perfectly, and purposefully, allowing the duck to take flight. The beak and feet are a cheery orange; the eyes are small glistening black circles. Recently, my daughter pointed out that a duck's beak by itself looks like a dog's head – it's uncanny really, and worth Googling. The entire duck package is spectacular.

Like the ducks, Thanksgiving is also something we've always had, and always will. We often enjoy it in a superficial way, neglecting to look beyond its surface. If we really examine it and revel in its meaning, we will experience its glory anew every year. It's a beautiful reminder of three things:

First, we need to remember to give thanks for all we have. So often we focus on what we don't have, or what we want. Or, we give thanks to God only when we're pleased with what is happening in our lives. The Pilgrims, even in the midst of hardships most of us cannot even fathom, remembered to thank God for their blessings. In everything, they gave thanks.

Second, not only did they give thanks, but they sat down together over a meal to do so. This is an extraordinary reminder for us. We need to remember the power of sitting down together over a table with family and friends. It is extremely hard during some seasons of our lives; when three kids have three different activities most evenings it's not easy to sit down together, much less assemble anything to put on the table. During those seasons don't despair; be realistic and try for one meal a week, or a few each month. Even a few meals together are better than none.

Third, we need to remember why the Pilgrims came here in the first place. They were fleeing religious persecution. They wanted the freedom to worship God their way, not the government's way. They left everything they had ever known to obtain this freedom. Their incredible passion for religious freedom is one of the foundations of this country. We should never take it for granted.

In everything, we should give thanks. And we should always insist that turkey is the bird we should be feasting upon; we should never, ever, eat a duck. Remember, Google "duck's beak looks like dog's head" if you need more persuading. You'll be even more convinced that ducks are fabulous.

A Christmas Pageant

D irecting a church Christmas pageant is not for the faint of heart.

Props are misplaced, mangers fall apart from overuse (often with a live baby Jesus within them) lines are forgotten, and tiny sheep panic and balk while crawling down the aisle. But the hardest part of the pageant is something that occurs before even one rehearsal. Without a doubt, the hardest part is casting the roles.

Casting is dicey because girls want to be Mary and boys want to be Joseph or one of the three kings. No one wants to be a shepherd, or an innkeeper, or the donkey. After all, these parts have very few — or in the donkey's case no — lines. But as we know, the show can't go on without shepherds and the manger scene.

With this in mind my pageant co-director and I sat at the kitchen table one December and agonized over assigning parts. How could we please everybody, children and parents? Was it possible to hurt no one's feelings? Was leaving town and returning after the New Year a viable option for us? We had six older girls who wanted to be Mary and three who wanted to be Elizabeth. Seven older boys wanted to be Joseph or a wise man. No matter how we sliced it someone would be disappointed. Feeling somewhat resigned, we put our heads down and got to work, and just before midnight assigned the last role.

Three days later our cast assembled for its first rehearsal. Excitement ran high. Eager faces looked at us expectantly. After giving a short pep talk about the importance of each and every role, we began assigning parts.

As each part was called, I watched the children's reactions closely. Some faces were alight with joy, some were downcast. One girl was fighting back tears; I cannot express how distressed that made me. Some of the younger children looked stunned and disbelieving. I understood why. They were being introduced to the tough concept of an uneven playing field. They had wanted a big part and had made that clear, but the more prominent roles went to the older kids, not the younger ones. This was the first time some of them had experienced a loss of some type; in park district sports like soccer, the younger teams don't keep score. No one wins, but no one loses; everyone is equal. That just doesn't hold true in real life. The pageant, appropriately enough, was a slice of real life.

Not only does real life throw us some curve balls, it's also, at least for most of us, quite ordinary. Most of us aren't famous but sometimes wish to be. Most of us are never credited with doing something extraordinary; rather, most of us live rather quietly, impacting others in ways we may never know. Most of us are not Mary or Joseph, but shepherds, guarding our flock of children and family to keep them from harm. We're humble compared to Hollywood superstars or powerful politicians, but no less important.

We must remind ourselves — and our children — of this fact. The Christmas story is a great way to do it. For example, so many girls yearn to be cast as Mary, an obviously pivotal role in our pageant of life. But who was she, really? She was an ordinary woman – faith-filled, no doubt — living an ordinary life, engaged to an ordinary man. Yet God chose her to bear his son. It's a perfect illustration of humbleness being used for greatness. Because of her faith, not her status or beauty, her name will be forever known. That's inspiring.

Many names in the Christmas story were never recorded. Even though the shepherds weren't named, they were among the first to witness a life-changing event. They went away full of wonder and reported the great thing they had seen. They played an important role 2000 years ago, and continue to have a vital role in our Christmas pageants. The innkeeper who offered the stable also remains nameless. But his humble contribution is evidenced in nativity scenes, Christmas carols, Christmas cards, and yes, Christmas pageants.

Ordinary people can indeed do great things.

The youngest children in the church were not yet concerned with status, only participation. They were beautiful to watch. Garbed in white sweatpants with black noses, they shuffled shyly down the aisle, bleating softly. Some were so excited they were trembling with the joy of it all. Their very young age facilitated their faith. They didn't want to be the star of the show. They just wanted to be included in the show.

Each Christmas, we should remember we're all invited to be part of the show. Jesus came for everyone, not only the famous, or powerful, or popular. We're all invited to partake in the gift of Jesus, not only on Christmas, but every day of our lives.

We should be trembling with joy while we participate.

The Real Gift

When my youngest daughter Grace was four, she was obsessed with Santa Claus.

That December her entire demeanor changed. She moved cautiously, spoke sweetly, and asked frequently throughout the Advent season: "Am I being a good girl?" She was convinced she was under constant surveillance by the big guy who distributed the loot, and she wanted to ensure she got her share. Her personality evolution was somewhat disquieting to me: there was no fighting with her brother, no dropping her clothes on the floor, no moaning about feeding the dog. She even offered to make her sister's bed, and as this bed was a top bunk this was no easy feat.

Her list for Santa was long and fluid. It was comprised of Polly Pocket accessories, Dora the Explorer houses and Barbie cars. Whenever we went to Target she would reverently hold each coveted toy, turning it around and around in her little hands and inspecting it closely. Each toy was more plastic and cheaply constructed than the next, but to her, they were perfect, and she was careful to cover her bases. "Will Santa make them just like this? Will the Dora house be made of this colorful stuff and not wood? It's not supposed to be made of wood. Maybe Santa should just get the stuff on my list at Target." In her mind, Santa's workshop created wooden toys on pull strings. These were not on her A list.

I remember having the same concern when I was four. How could Santa make my Easy Bake oven? I wanted that actual sophisticated piece of equipment, not some wooden substitute from Santa. My mother assured me that Santa also got toys from stores, and that's exactly what I told my daughter during that Christmas season: Santa does shop at stores that little girls and boys like. Yes, he still makes his own toys. But shopping in stores saves him time. After all, think of all the new babies we know. Every day he has more and more children to visit. These assurances seemed to calm her but I knew her well enough to know her little mind was still envisioning her Barbie Car might look like something her brother built for the Pinewood Derby.

That December Grace saw Santa. No, I did not wait in line for two hours with hundreds of sobbing children at the nearby mall; even I had my limits. Santa was installed in a huge, throne-like chair (very appropriate in Grace's eyes) in the middle of my husband's company Christmas party. Every child was invited to sit on Santa's lap for a picture and a present. My daughter's eyes were like saucers; she bravely marched up to him and practically catapulted onto his lap. She offered a sweet smile, smoothed her dress and launched into a barely discernible account of presents, her guinea pig, and her recent angelic behavior. Oh, the self-assurance of a last-born! When my eldest daughter was four, she sat mute and terrified on Santa's lap.

After receiving a present from Santa (Glory be! A Dora the Explorer sleeping bag!) our youngest marched back to us, beaming.

Santa had delivered. She had been a bit surprised he had asked her what she wanted for Christmas; hadn't she written him a letter explaining about the Barbie car and Polly Pockets? She had helped address the envelope and had even included an extra page of drawings she had done for him. Do you think he had read it?

Of course he read it, we assured her. He's just asking to make sure you didn't forget anything when you wrote your letter. She seemed to accept this explanation and dug into her ice cream, temporarily satisfied.

As we drove home I pondered the Santa situation. I was uneasy, feeling like we were going a bit overboard with our baby. After all, in our household we really drive home that Christmas is about Jesus. He's our gift, the best one we could imagine. I knew my older two children had always understood that, even when they believed in Santa. To them, Santa was always secondary to the tiny baby born in a manger. I was becoming a bit uncertain about my Miss Greedy Pants.

Don't get me wrong. I love Santa and everything he represents. When the time comes when Santa is not expected in our household, I'll mourn that loss. But looking in the back seat at my daughter blissfully caressing her Dora sleeping bag made me pause. Maybe we had gone too far with her. It would probably be a good thing to re-clarify what Christmas truly was all about.

Later that night, when my daughter was safely ensconced in her new sleeping bag, I sat on the floor next to her. I began talking about what Christmas really was, and why we celebrated it. She interrupted me, not rudely, but matter-of-factly. "I know, I know Mom. Santa only comes because Jesus came first." I agreed that was the case. "Without Jesus," she continued, "Santa wouldn't know what I wanted. Jesus tells him." I was so startled I couldn't think of a reply.

My daughter continued, her words beginning to blur with sleepiness. "Jesus knows what I want because He lives inside me. He's part of me; He lives in my heart, and He talks to me, and Santa too. I listen to Him, and Santa listens to Him."

Okay, so it's not perfect theology. But it quickened my heart. I believe my daughter will grow up to be a joyful Christian, because she has Jesus in her center and she trusts Him to take care of her.

I went to bed smiling.

Chapter 7: Grace In Dumpsters & Dust

"One of the advantages of being disorganized is that one is always having surprising discoveries."

— A.A. Milne

Picturing Our Blessings

In my house, pictures are everywhere.

These pictures aren't in frames. They're not in albums. They're not even in stacks. Instead, they're pushed between books, stuffed in junk drawers, and stacked with magazines. They're pressed in the glove compartment of the car, tucked in the toolbox in the garage, and balanced on the front hall closet shelf. Pictures abound, yet when I'm looking for one they're nowhere to be found. Somehow, once the pictures are ordered or printed from my computer, they fall into the picture hole that is my residence.

That's why I jumped at the chance to attend a neighborhood scrapbooking evening. Even though craft projects usually strike terror into my heart, I was assured that creating memorable scrapbooks was a breeze. In fact, the very first step was simply putting all of my pictures in sequential order. We were told to bring pictures to sort and organize. That – and laughter — were the evening's only goals. I was in.

I went about the monumental task of gathering pictures into a large Rubbermaid box. When I had finished, I couldn't snap on the lid; they were absolutely mounded. Still, I had them all in one spot for the first time in years. That in itself was a success.

When the evening arrived, I somewhat shamefacedly brought my overflowing bin to the organizing festivities. As I walked in the house, I immediately felt better. People were arriving with dresser drawers crammed with pictures, bags stuffed with pictures, and containers with their lids secured with bungee cords. I felt right at home.

We all began sorting through our stacks. I felt a rush of adrenaline; never again would I get this behind in chronicling my life. I almost gleefully pulled out a stack of photos and started the task of sorting them.

The first picture was easy to place. It was my daughter's first day of kindergarten. That meant it needed to be placed in the Fall/Winter pile. So far, so good. The second picture caused me to falter. It was an adorable shot of my middle child, but I had no idea when it was taken, and held it up for inspection. "Guys, how old do you think Rhett was here?" I asked. Several people looked the photo over.

"He was one," someone stated.

"No, he looks way older than one," someone else insisted. "He was at least two there!"

"Is there any sort of decoration in the background?" another woman asked hopefully. "Do you see any pumpkins, or garland? That will help you place it."

We all squinted at the picture, to no avail. No clues loomed in the background; I was stuck, and only on picture number two. I looked at his cute little boy sweater and realized it was a hand-me-down from my neighbor. Success! If she remembered when she gave me the sweater, perhaps I could give the picture a date. "Hey Mary" I asked, "do you remember when you passed this sweater along to Rhett?"

Mary took the picture and pondered it a bit. "Maybe two falls ago?" she hazarded. Another neighbor looked over her shoulder. "That would have been way more than two years ago! Phillip got that sweater for his third birthday! He hasn't worn it for years!" The picture consultant who was hosting the evening sensed trouble and swooped over to me. "If you're unsure, put it in the unsure pile," she said authoritatively. "Don't get bogged down! Keep moving forward!" I took her advice and plunged my arm into the Rubbermaid container to pull out another stack.

As the evening wore on, I began enjoying myself more and more. I found that I was astounded at pictures of my own children. Were they really ever that little? Despite being in a house with ten other women, I began traveling down my own memory lane, and was at times miles away.

A picture of us around the dining room table brought me back to Thanksgiving dinner several years ago. We spent the day with three other couples who are very dear to us. Gazing at those forgotten photos, memories of that day came rushing back to greet me. One showed the cooked turkey in all its glory (it was the first time I had made a turkey myself and I wanted proof I had actually done it), another of my daughter as a baby with sweet potatoes smeared in her hair. A third showed all eight of us toasting to our first Thanksgiving together. My eyes stung with tears; that was indeed our first Thanksgiving together, but unbeknownst to us at the time, it was also our last. Two of the couples have since moved away, making me doubly grateful I had unearthed these pictures at last.

Another picture chronicled hundreds of pieces of wood lying on the bedroom floor, and I remembered the day we set up bunk beds for our daughters. When the bunk beds were showcased in IKEA assembly seemed like it would be ridiculously simple, but when we unpacked the long flat boxes we were overwhelmed, and took pictures so we would always remember the beds looked like Lincoln Logs before they looked like beds. Oh, what a long evening it was putting them together! But it was a fun one.

I remembered the first day we got our dog. I found the picture of him curled in my daughter's lap the very first night he came home. He was the quintessential Golden Retriever puppy: fuzzy and fat, with a perfect little pointy tail. He's now so sleek and big I had forgotten how tasty he was when he was little.

My stacks grew slowly, but my memories and emotions were mounting up much faster. I was becoming overwhelmed by a feeling I could not name until much later. It was, quite simply, gratitude. God has blessed my family in incredible ways.

I shouldn't have to look through pictures to remember that, I know. But somehow, pictures of our lives help our often weak and tired minds remember what we already know. God is good. And so is this life.

There's no better reason to start organizing our stacks of pictures. If pictures help us count our blessings, so be it. But that means we need to pull them out of hiding or print them off our computers so we can see them. They can help remind us that God is always —even in our tiny lives— at work.

Pillars of Piles

My daughter Clara sauntered into the kitchen, dressed and ready for school. I looked up from pouring juice and stared in astonishment. She was wearing a shirt that didn't cover her belly and shorts that didn't cover her behind. The entire ensemble was inappropriate, yet there was something familiar about it, as if I'd seen it before.

Something clicked. I had indeed seen the outfit before – we had bought it last year, and it had completely covered her belly as well as her behind. Then, it had been darling and one of my daughter's favorite outfits. Now, it was bordering on indecent. I sighed, gearing up for the fight that was certain to come. With a calmness I didn't feel I told my daughter the outfit no longer fit her, and she needed to change. "But Mom!" she argued, "This is one of my favorite outfits and I haven't had it in a long time. But this morning it was in a pile in my room! That's why I thought it was okay to put on!"

I assured her she had chosen from the wrong pile. There were piles of clothes she could wear, and piles she could not wear. "Then why are the clothes I cannot wear piled in my room?" she asked, not unreasonably.

This logical question had a logical answer: I was using her room because I needed every inch of space for my piles. Clothes were everywhere because I was pulling out summer clothes and storing winter clothes. At first, this task seems straightforward. But as it progresses, difficulties mount. Clothes stored away at the end of last summer are now too small. Overlooked spots and stains on packed away clothes seem somehow glaring. And what should I do with the winter clothes that are already on the small side? Decisions abound, and piles grow.

There are piles of clothes in every bedroom. There are piles of clothes in the office, piles in the hallway, and piles on chairs. There are piles to give to Goodwill, piles to give to good friends, and piles to pack away for good memories. There are stacks of clothes outgrown by one daughter but not yet ready for the second daughter. There are mounds of winter clothes that need to be sorted into further piles – clothes that have a chance of being worn next winter, clothes that have a chance to be worn in two winters, and clothes with so many stains they need to be permanently shelved. Adding to this cluster is the unsteady stack of huge Rubbermaid containers waiting to be filled, labeled and stored.

When everything is sorted into piles and the piles are labeled, the major extraction begins. Bags of clothes are stuffed into my husband's car for their trip to Goodwill. Different bags are stuffed into my car to be dropped at various locations with small children. Smaller bags contain special outfits that have been borrowed and now need to be returned. The Rubbermaid containers are filled, labeled, and stashed in the attic. This stashing is no easy feat. Our attic does not boast a staircase, only pull down steps that can hit you on the head and knock you out if you're not careful. I've learned to pull them down while jumping reflexively to the right. Once they're down, I ascend these ladder-like stairs hoisting bulky, heavy Rubbermaid containers which I'm careful to place on the floor joists only, or they'll merely drop down through the ceiling back into the bedrooms.

By the time I get everything sorted out for the season, the season is changing. It tends to get a bit depressing. But the good thing about not having enough clothes storage is that every season I feel as if I have a new wardrobe. I root through storage containers I packed up only six months before and revel in clothes I forgot I had. So, there is an upswing to the whole process.

My daughter did go back upstairs that day to change, but only after I showed her which piles were off-limits and which were acceptable to root through. It took me a few minutes to determine that myself, actually. I understand her initial excitement about finding her outgrown outfit once again; it's hard for kids to give up their favorite outfits. I thought about my absolute favorite vest I got when I was six. It was crocheted in sky blue wool with a fat white stripe – quintessential seventies stuff. I adored it and was devastated when my mom retired it, telling me I had grown so much it was now too short to wear. I probably wore it only one season; being able to wear your favorite pieces year after year is one of the few perks of getting older. When I look at pictures of myself in that vest I still think it looked cool.

I need to remember, as I plunge into my semi-annual clothes sorting frenzy, that even as I wish for larger closets, I'm quite rich indeed. God has given me three healthy children who outgrow their clothes at a good clip. Shirts become too short, pants too tight, and shoes too small. That's something we often consider an expensive nuisance, but it's really a blessing. I need to thank Him for this gift – and therefore my piles – every day.

The Dumpster

In a short few years, doing laundry in my house had evolved from a tedious chore into a dangerous expedition. My washer and dryer rested in the back corner of my hundred-year-old basement, barely discernible in the gloom. To get to this back corner, we gingerly picked our way through a myriad of obstacles balancing a full laundry basket. This minefield consisted of normal things you would find in any respectable unfinished basement: paint cans, chairs without seats, broken ping pong tables, unused water softeners, and old college textbooks. Like the American pioneers before us, we broke a trail through this wilderness to reach our destination – in this case, our clean clothes.

One day, while struggling to the laundry area, I noticed the path to cleanliness seemed narrower. Since my clothes still fit, I discarded the possibility I was growing and considered the equally unattractive possibility that the path was shrinking. This meant that more things had found their way into the already stuffed back room of our basement. I dismissed the thought almost immediately – it just wasn't possible.

Then, out of the blue one evening, my husband suggested we call for a dumpster. I blinked. Maybe he decided to remodel the kitchen after all. I'd better get busy emptying our ancient kitchen cabinets, in that case. And, I'd have to take down all the window treatments; they were just made and I did not want them full of drywall dust. "Are we ready to demolish the kitchen?" I asked hopefully.

He gave me a disbelieving look. "The basement," he clarified. "We'll get a big one, a twenty yarder. That way, we can clear everything out no problem, and we can let our neighbors throw some things out too. We'll let them know it's coming so they can figure out what they want to get rid of. Everyone will be glad to use it."

Generous as this sentiment was, it did not thrill me. Filling a dumpster didn't sound like a great way to spend a weekend, especially a beautiful autumn weekend. I'd been planning to take the kids to the zoo; the weather was supposed to be perfect. Why not just fill up a few extra garbage cans and call it a day? And we could place large pieces out on the curb on garbage day – they were always snatched up immediately. What would we do with a twenty yard dumpster? It would take up our whole driveway, and we wouldn't even use half of it. Plus, it was expensive. I looked my husband almost twitching with the excitement of it all, bit my tongue and ordered the dumpster.

When it arrived all my fears were realized. It was gargantuan, it was smelly, and it banished our cars to the street. I gazed at it for a while before going inside to call my husband at work. "It's arrived!" I pronounced when he answered. I might have been announcing the birth of a niece or nephew.

The following morning, the christening of the dumpster began. At first it was fun, even therapeutic, to toss items helter-skelter into the cavernous metal box. As my husband suspected, there was no shortage of fodder to feed into the dumpster. We threw away old dehumidifiers, an ancient water softener, college level philosophy books, and decaying bookshelves. I was surprised at how quickly the dumpster seemed to be filling up; perhaps my husband was right to insist on such a large one.

While we purged, we reminisced and laughed. We tossed in rolls of duck wallpaper border (purchased when country was in!) from our very first house, a tiny two bedroom ranch. It was – literally — the cheapest house on the market when we were house hunting, and we jumped on it. We considered ourselves the luckiest people in Wheaton when we bought it. And we remembered our second home, a home we suspected was a Sears Catalog Kit home, though we never found proof of that. When we bought that house we also acquired two wooden chairs held together with glue, an old stove with porcelain knobs and a gigantic roasting pot. We were thrilled with our treasures, and vowed to repair the chairs and stove and restore the pot. We never did; we only moved them from house to house. These things also found their way into the dumpster. We unearthed boxes of yearbooks from junior high and high school we had forgotten about, and spent time sorting through them, laughing and exclaiming. Those we kept.

The fun started to diminish when we realized the dumpster was very close to being full. Not only full, but mounded, which is a strict taboo in garbage land. Refuse must be level with the top of the container. We re-arranged, stomped, and shoved to level off our pile. We stuck old cross country skis into the crevices, gave the entire thing one last kick, and slammed the gate shut.

Thinking back, I think filling the dumpster was a snap for us because we were ready for transition. We were ready, as a family, to embark on a new stage of our lives together. We felt settled, yet somehow excited. Where God would lead us we didn't know, but we did know we no longer needed to save old chairs or textbooks as reminders of our past. We were looking toward the future.

It's amazing how good you feel when you de-clutter and organize – I felt as though I had a new house. The narrow path in the basement had turned into an open field of concrete floors and cinder block walls, and getting to my washer and dryer was now a walk in the park. Telling our neighbors we didn't have room for their piece of drywall in our twenty yard dumpster was not.

A Container Christmas

Anything's possible with the right container.

This epiphany struck me four days before Christmas, while I was rooting through my packed front hall closet in search of wrapping paper. I discovered crayons, rubber bands, baseball bats, one snow boot, three mittens, a pair of socks, a box of nails, and a crumpled magazine. I finally found a roll of wrapping paper wedged in the dark back corner of the closet, crushed and unusable.

There had to be a better way to store things in my tiny closets, I thought despondently. I loved my old farmhouse, but those early settlers were not big on closet space.

I grabbed the mangled magazine from the closet floor and absently leafed through it. My eyes widened as page after page of perfect linen closets, organized front hall closets, and debris-free entryways shone out at me. The featured modest closets were full of clear neatly labeled boxes, the small entryways boasted hall benches and sturdy wicker baskets. Here was proof that even with non-existent storage, organization was possible. You just needed the right equipment.

(This equipment was not cheap. But, I reasoned, how can one put a price on ease of life?)

All the pictured organizational goodies had clear instructions on where to buy them. I put tabs on every page and circled each item in red pen. There! My husband had been asking me what I wanted for Christmas. Now, I had my Christmas list.

That night, leafing through my wish list, my husband's face fell. "What's this thing with the pockets? Where will that go?" I assured him it would effortlessly organize our closets.

"Well, what is a wrapping paper organizer? Why do we need to organize wrapping paper anyway? Don't we already keep it in the front hall closet? I don't want to give you this stuff," he protested. "I want to get you something more personal. This won't be any fun for me."

I reminded him he had begged me for gift ideas, and I had come through. These glorious containers were all I wanted for Christmas. They might not be fun for him to give, but they would be fun for me to receive. I showed him the photo of the perfectly aligned front hall closet to close the sale.

"See! Look at this closet! You can open the door and things won't fall on top of you. Wouldn't this be great? We could actually hang up guests' coats!" I was working all possible angles. My husband shrugged. He did not seem impressed.

Christmas morning I was delighted to unwrap canvas bins, a wrapping paper organizer, and my clear multi-pocket shoe holder the magazine had touted as indispensable. I could stuff every pocket with the junk that usually winds up as flotsam in any house – hair bands, paper clips, rubber bands, glue, tape, pliers, felt sticky pads, and Goo Gone. I'd have all my junk neatly organized.

I was especially excited about the wrapping paper holder. The whole concept seemed too good to be true. You could neatly store up to ten rolls of wrapping paper in one vertical snap-tight container. Never again would my wrapping paper be rumpled. Never again would I search for a bow. I was about to embark on a new phase of organizational life. I grabbed three rolls of Christmas wrap and dropped them in the holder.

They didn't fit. They loomed almost six inches over the top. Because they were too long, I couldn't put the top on. And when I couldn't put the top on, I couldn't store my bows and tags. I was devastated. I realized the holder was not created to store jumbo rolls of wrapping paper, which is all I buy.

A week later, I returned the wrapping container, got my refund, and browsed around the store. There were hundreds of different types of containers, including a half dozen wrapping paper containers. My spirits lifted. Maybe one of these would work. I carefully compared them and chose one a good six inches longer than the rest. Surely, it would do the trick.

When I rushed home and tried it, the wrapping paper rolls were still inches too long.

All was not lost. I did have one round container, one desk container, and three fabric covered boxes to play with. You see, when I returned the original wrapping container, I did make a few additional purchases. They were sitting in the store in rows, tempting as chocolate. I was looking forward to filling them up and savoring them.

I also still technically owned my second wrapping paper container; instead of wrapping paper, it now held my son's Lincoln Logs. I often went into his room to glance wistfully at it —wishing it was mine.

So often we ask for gifts because we think they will in some way improve our lives. When we actually receive the gift, it seldom lives up to the promise. It simply never works like it does on the commercial, or organizes like it does in the glossy pages of Martha Stewart's magazine. Just like my wrapping paper holder, gifts that are too good to be true often are, and may not work for us no matter how hard we try.

It's a good thing our ultimate gift was given to us by the One who is perfect. This gift will never disappoint us. We don't even need to ask for it; we need only to accept it. It's already been given to us, after all. When we do accept it, we may remain unorganized, but our lives will be improved, often in ways we could never expect.

Chapter 8: The Blessing Of Friendships

"Friendship is unnecessary, like philosophy, like art... It has no survival value; rather it is one of those things that give value to survival."

—*C.S. Lewis*

The Foosball Table

When we were first married my husband and I rented a small one-bedroom apartment. It had a balcony, an eat-in kitchen, white walls and non-descript carpeting. We thought it was paradise.

We proudly set up our few possessions, most of them kindly donated by older, more established family members. We had no dining room set, but we did have a foosball table that filled the dining area nicely. We didn't have matching kitchen chairs, but we did have a sturdy kitchen table that originated from a dormitory lounge area at Southern Illinois University. It's still unclear how we obtained the table; neither of us attended SIU. Regardless, it was handy, and quite heavy.

Our living room was pure 1980's. Two shiny satin white couches flanked a black lacquer coffee table topped with mirrors. The couches looked fine, but were almost impossible to sit on. Once you perched on one, you slid right off onto the floor. They were that slippery. We overcame this obstacle by covering the gleaming satin with rather grungy afghans we had inherited from our grandmothers. The afghans, though they ruined the sleek look we were aiming for, did keep us from sliding off the couches and therefore remained in all their mustard and olive green crocheted glory. Still, we were thrilled with our living room; the couches and the afghans were free, and that was the magic word.

I worked as a publishing sales representative during those days and while my home office was in Baltimore I was based in Chicago. My office was at home, and consisted of an old door laid on top of a pair of double drawer file cabinets. This make-shift desk shared the dining room area with the foosball table. The medical textbooks I sold were stacked along the walls, along with crates of coffee mugs promoting an anatomy atlas, sheaves of free highlighters for students, and stacks of paperweights emblazoned with our company logo.

I'm remembering our first home because it was the location of our debut annual Christmas party, which my husband and I recently just hosted once again for the 21st time. We've held it every year, in good years and in harder years, through recessions, new babies, new jobs and new houses. The parties have been a blast every year but that first Christmas party is still my favorite. The apartment was decorated with a few strands of white lights around my desk and our first Christmas tree. The tree was pretty bare because we didn't have many ornaments, but I remember it smelled incredible.

That party centered around our new Elvis Blue Christmas CD and the foosball table. Things got pretty loud. In fact, now that I really think about it, the noise level was probably not appropriate. People were jumping up and down whenever they scored a goal; they were stomping their feet when they missed a ball, they were dancing around to Elvis while awaiting their turn at the foosball table. The tenants underneath us pounded their ceiling with a broom handle in a vain attempt to quiet us down.

Much has changed since that party 20 years ago. We now live in a house, not an apartment, and we no longer have a balcony. I have a dining table, not a foosball table, in my dining room. I still have a home office, but it no longer consists of an old door and filing cabinets. Things have evolved, certainly. But something very important to us, then and now, has remained constant. The core group of people we surrounded ourselves with back then is still the same. For this, I am very grateful.

Our most recent Christmas party went very late. My husband and I insisted we truly weren't tired; of course people were welcome to stay. And people did. The same group who gathered in our first apartment twenty years ago were the ones who stayed until it was almost light. The only exception was one newer friend who, although she didn't share our history together, somehow fit in as though she did.

An aside – I think that's often the case. As we grow older and make new friends, we know ourselves well enough to choose them for the right reasons. Usually, our new friends we cultivate and our older friends we cherish have much in common. We've just met them at different times.

As I was laughing so much my sides hurt, I was suddenly overwhelmed with a feeling I couldn't identify. It was one I enjoyed, and it had a faintly familiar feeling. I tried to examine it — to poke and prod at it a bit — but the commotion around me made reflection impossible.

It wasn't until weeks later that I put my finger on how I – and I believe all of us – were feeling that night. In our hearts, we were feeling young. We were bursting, once again, with that invincible feeling you thrive upon in your early twenties. Back then, despite having almost no money between us, and even fewer possessions, we felt rich, utterly rich.

We thought life couldn't get any better. After all, we had each other, a foosball table, and a balcony. We were getting ready to launch our lives, our marriages, and our careers. We thought we had the world by the tail.

And we did. We really did.

These almost surreal feelings of contentment and well-being have nothing to do with material wealth, or lack of it. They come from being with and depending on true friends. My husband and I started our married life together very modestly. But we were — and still remain — very, very rich in friends. We've all come a long way since that foosball-saturated first Christmas gathering. We have hoards of children, triumphs, and heartbreaks between us, but we are all still together in good times and in bad.

True friends are one of God's greatest gifts to us, and like His gift of grace, they are free. We just need to accept them.

The foosball table finally fell apart several years ago. My husband and I retired it to the curb, and watched as some excited teenagers scraped it up and put it in the back of their car. I hope they can piece it back together, just as we did when we pulled it off another Wheaton curb, so many years ago.

Making Time for Friends

T he holidays are officially over. Abandoned, dried Christmas trees rest forlornly at the curbs. The nativity set is safely packed away; the garland that adorned our windows is now decorating the back room of our basement. Wrapping paper has been retrieved from underneath the couch, and most of the new toys are either missing pieces or broken. Another January begins.

That means I'm once again pondering my life-long New Year's resolution. It never changes because I've never achieved it. It's a simple one really. My ongoing New Year's resolution is to spend more quality time with my family and friends.

Sounds easy enough, doesn't it? But somehow, as the year marches on, it becomes more complicated. There's always something to be done that interferes with my well-intended resolution. Columns need to be written, kids need to be transported, groceries need to be purchased, classes need to be prepared for and taught. Topping off this laundry list is a retriever who needs more walks, a guinea pig who needs a clean cage, and a rabbit who needs her nails cut. Thankfully the hermit crabs and goldfish are low maintenance. Why I'm running a small zoo here I don't know, but it doesn't help me with my time-management problem one bit.

A task-filled life is nothing new for most of us. Whether we're young or old, married or single, we have things in our lives we must accomplish. That's not going to change. But somehow, things we *must* accomplish often entirely crowd out the things we *should* accomplish, like visiting with those we love. We tend to place relationships at the bottom of our long to-do list.

I always picture the illustration that's overused yet somehow powerful: if you have a glass jar you must fill with rocks, the best way to do that is by putting the largest rocks into the jar first. That way, you ensure they have room. The little rocks can squeeze their way in using the space around the big rocks. The big rocks of course represent things most important to you – put them first, this illustration tells you, and everything else will follow. The big rocks should be our relationships, certainly. They so often are shelved while we focus on what we think is important. Yet when I reflect on this past year, the highlights are times I spent with those closest to me. That's why I make my resolution every year. I want to keep focusing on spending time with those I love.

I have a long way to go, but I can see definite progress in my perpetual New Year's resolution. When I think of the best times in the prior year, they almost all took place in my family room. During the crazy month of December alone, I can fondly replay many hours of couch time holding babies and conversations. I remember sometimes worrying during these visits (laundry was sitting in the washer, presents needed to be wrapped, and writing deadlines loomed) but consciously shelving the worry so it didn't interfere with the moment.

I had a wonderful month full of coffee and conversations, laughter and occasional tears. I cannot recall, however, what pressing tasks I completed after the visits were over. They simply did not make any impression at all.

The rewarding December visits all had one thing in common – they were impromptu. The chance for a visit was there, and it was jumped on. Usually, dog hair was everywhere, I was in exercise clothes, and the breakfast dishes were still in the sink. No one cared. No one wanted anything but a chance to unwind and talk about things important to them, or perhaps not so important. I've slowly become more relaxed about welcoming people into my home, even when things are in disarray.

I have several friends who put me to shame in the visiting department. They're stop-by people, ones who show up unannounced, and expect others to do the same. They don't care what their house looks like, or what they're in the middle of. They'll welcome you joyfully —with open arms —no matter when or why you drop in. I don't know if I'll ever attain the generous gift of hospitality they have. But I find it interesting that I seem to be attracted to people with that gift. Perhaps I need their calming influence in my life.

Throughout this year, as I plod along with my resolution in mind, I'm going to focus on my December visits. I'm going to remember how they made me feel – fulfilled, calm, and thankful. I'm going to remember I somehow made the time for them to happen, even during the busiest month of the year. I'm going to remember that I can't recall what I set aside to make these visits happen. And I'm going to remember that life here is short.

No one, at their life's end, wishes for more time to clean their bathrooms. What they do wish for is more time with the ones they love. This year, we can make that wish come true.

When Jesus was here on this earth He was almost always surrounded by the ones He loved. Somehow, He still got quite a lot accomplished, didn't He?

Reunion Reality

Expectations often leave us disappointed or at the very least, somewhat bereft.

That's because they're our own man-made scenarios of what's going to happen. Because God is ultimately in charge, our expectations about almost any event just don't match reality. We lack the vision or perhaps (and this is my take entirely) the sense of humor He has. Not surprisingly, we often discover that the reality we experience, though as different from our expectations as night is from day, actually outshines our expectations. My fifteen-year college reunion was a perfect example of this.

About a month prior to the reunion, I received an enthusiastic phone call from one of my college friends. We should go to Augustana's homecoming this fall, she insisted. Just the six of us — no husbands, no children. After all, it was our fifteen-year reunion. We didn't see each other enough; this would be the perfect excuse to spend a weekend together. Plus, she pointed out, we hadn't seen most of our sorority sisters since we graduated. This reunion would be the time to reconnect and reestablish dear relationships that we had let slip.

I glanced at my calendar. The homecoming weekend in question already looked crammed. But then I started thinking about it. When would there be a good weekend? If we waited until we were all free, a reunion weekend would never happen. As it was our 15th reunion, there would be hoards of people there from our class; it would be great to see them. Our graduating class was about 600 people. I knew most of them would not make the trip, but if even 50 did . . . it would be a great time. I had lost track of most of them, as my girlfriend had so firmly pointed out. It was time to rectify that, so I decided to go, as did my girlfriends.

As we drove to the Quad Cities we hatched a plan. We would, we decided, meet up with people at the homecoming football game and at the gatherings sure to be held throughout the afternoon. The evening, however, we'd reserve for ourselves. It would be hard to break away from the crowds, but we resolved to manage it and have a nice dinner together, just the six of us. After our strategy was completed, we spent the rest of the car ride trying to remember names. "Remember the tall guy with blond hair in the PUBA fraternity? What was his name? What about that girl who was such an incredible piano player? She was Student Council President; she'll definitely be back. Why can't I remember her name? Jane? Jen?"

I was especially concerned about placing people and names; it is definitely not my strength. I was having bad images of holding long conversations at the football game without ever figuring out who I was talking to. It's happened before.

When we arrived on campus we headed straight to the football game to find our fellow classmates. After a brief skirmish over ticket prices (no free tickets for alumni?) we strode in, shoulders back, smiles on our faces, tingling with self-awareness. Did we look much older? Would people even recognize us? We slowly walked toward the end zone, pricking our ears in case people called to us from the stands. No one did.

We reached the mobs of people standing in the end zone. While we wove through them, we noticed much hugging and crying. People were back for the weekend and reconnecting. We were also ready to reconnect. As we inspected the huggers, we noticed most of them seemed over fifty or under twenty-five. We wove through the crowd for several minutes before the truth hit us. We would not have to worry about remembering names, or affiliations, or hometowns.

We knew no one.

Even as this reality dawned, we refused to give up hope. We spotted an impossibly young girl wearing our sorority letters and introduced ourselves. When we mentioned our pledging year her eyes widened slightly. We asked what sorority alumni activities were planned for the weekend, and were rewarded with a bright smile. "Welcome!" she chirped. "Wow, you guys graduated a long time ago! No, nothing's planned for alumni. Have a great weekend, though."

So much for that.

Perhaps, one of our group ventured, everyone's at Lee's. Lee's was the hangout spot while we were at Augustana. If you ever wanted to find people, you went there. We agreed that was a possibility, left the game and piled back into the car. We drove to Lee's, a trip we could have made blindfolded. Except Lee's wasn't there anymore. Lee's was now a car wash.

This was beyond the realm of our comprehension. Where was the new meeting spot? How could we be back at this place where we were so involved, and feel so adrift? This was not the plan.

But it was our reality. And after a few minutes, we decided to accept it. When we did, we had an absolutely fantastic time.

We reacquainted ourselves with the campus. We all had certain buildings we wanted to reconnect with. Mine was the English building, with the worn old marble steps and the stained glass windows. It was just as beautiful as I remembered, and it smelled just the same. Even the temperature in the building hadn't changed. The stairwell was stifling, the classrooms cool.

We visited our dorms and our sorority house. We reminisced in the old library, built over 100 years ago, and admired the new library, built the year after we graduated. We walked around every inch of the campus. It was ablaze with fiery orange and yellow maples, and the signature black squirrels were friskier than ever. It was a perfect time of year to be back.

We never did see anyone we knew. But we were together again, and that's all that really mattered. We had a new set of memories we could laugh over in the future, and that made the trip entirely worthwhile. The weekend gave us all what we needed, but not what we expected.

The Evolution of Life

A picture says a thousand words is a true statement indeed. As I gazed at a 1986 photograph of my sorority pledge class, I remembered anew the security of that time. Like all Greek groups on campus, we met Wednesday evenings to discuss what we considered important sorority business, and this informal snapshot was taken during one of those meetings. What struck me about the photo was not the big hair or the Forenza sweaters, but the countenance of my pledge class. We looked serene, young, and incredibly happy.

As we were in the midst of pledging, we looked identical as baby ducklings. Swathed in pale pink sorority shirts, pledge pins and pledge books, we were nestled together at the very front of the room, radiating security and well-being. We were never alone. Not only did we have each other, but we also had sixty older girls who were — from the moment we pledged — our instant teachers, big sisters and caretakers. They pampered and petted us, giving us cards, presents and candy for completing even the smallest pledging activity. More importantly, most were incredible role models for us.

It was a wonderful spring for my pledge class. The world was our oyster; anything was possible and every day was exciting. Sitting among us in the picture were our two pledge moms, older sorority sisters whom we depended upon for just about everything. They encouraged us when we were down and spent hours helping us study for both college and pledging requirements. They modeled college life for us in positive ways, showing us how to have fun with grace and class. They were always there for us, always laughing, and always on target. They were who we wanted to be when we grew up.

This snapshot from twenty years ago was displayed at the memorial service for one of those pledge moms. Her life ended tragically and prematurely at forty. Like twenty years before, I was with my pledge sisters, and like twenty years before, we felt confidence in simply being together. As a group, we could endure this death of our beloved pledge mom; we could not have borne it alone.

We were fortified from gathering together the previous evening and spending the night together. We had eaten, laughed, cried and reminisced. As the hours passed our conversation gradually became more introspective, and in the early morning hours, one of us asked the $60,000 question: If we could go back and change our pasts, would we? If we would change anything, what would it be?

I'd looked around the table and wondered what I would hear. We certainly had experienced hardships since those carefree pledging days; it would not be surprising to hear someone admit they would like to change the past. After all, one of us had lost her husband in a tragic accident after only two years of marriage. They had met and dated in college, and we had all stood up in their wedding. Another had a special needs child; yet another was in the midst of navigating a rather messy divorce. And of course on our minds was the memorial service we would be attending for our pledge mom. Her last few years had not been good ones. Would any of us change our past if we could? Everyone looked at everyone else, and we all answered the same way.

The answer was unequivocally no. We wouldn't. Even my pledge sister who found herself a widow at twenty-four agreed: great good had come from tragedy. My widowed friend eventually remarried and has three beautiful children. My friend with a special needs child wouldn't trade him for the world; she loves him without reserve. My divorcing friend has three incredible children from that ill-fated marriage; they wouldn't be who they are if they had a different father. As to our pledge mom, we couldn't make any sense of her premature death, but agreed we didn't have to make sense of it then, or maybe ever. God is in charge; he will make good come out of the sorrow, whether we recognize it or not.

We all agreed on that, and then agreed on something else. We were very grateful that when we first became friends at eighteen we didn't know our futures. We didn't then, and we shouldn't now. Much of what's in store for us may bring us great joy, but one thing's for sure. Not everything in our futures will be easy, enjoyable, or even tolerable. That we can't see ahead is a blessing, one we should always count.

At the memorial service the next day, gazing at the picture of our eighteen-year-old selves sprawled like exuberant puppies, I felt my throat tighten with tears. I was grateful our faces were open, innocent, and trusting. Grateful that we couldn't see ahead to our hard times. Grateful that we were blessed with our 18-year-old time of invincibility. Do I wish myself back to that spring of 1986? No. Am I glad we had it? You bet.

I've had many other periods of well-being in my life and hope for many more, but nothing can parallel the innocence of that spring. Yet I don't look back in a yearning sense, but rather a reflective one. Life evolves as you can handle it. While our innocence has dissolved, our friendships have not. Unlike innocence, friends can last forever.

Friends to the End

My daughter Clara came to me wearing an expression of weary six-year-old resignation.

"Mom, Susan and Emma are fighting again! Susan wants us to watch the dance she made up, and Emma refuses to do it. So now Susan is locked in the bathroom."

I shut down my laptop and went to diffuse this very common situation. I knocked on the bathroom door, coaxed out a teary Susan, and sat her down with an unrepentant Emma. I started soothing both parties by explaining to Emma that her opinion and attention was very important to Susan, and then I explained — once again — to Susan that Emma liked to climb trees, not watch dances. It wasn't personal; it was just Emma. Clara joined me in playing peacemaker, and eventually the situation resolved itself.

That was ten years ago, but I was remembering the scene rather wistfully the other night as I sat huddled on the bleachers at a high school football game. I was thrilled to be there and watch the successes and growth of the children I had known since preschool, yet I was melancholy as well. There were just so many changes.

Gone were the days of bathroom sulks and High School Musical parties. My daughter and her friends were knee-deep in sophomore year, juggling incredibly challenging classes while pursuing their interests. Not surprisingly, Susan is on the dance team. Clara is in show choir and drama, and Emma's first love is the swim team. I watched Susan step out on the football field during halftime to give her performance. She caught my gaze and gave me a cheery wave before bounding out with her squad.

I sighed inwardly. Although change is a part of life —especially parenthood —a piece of me has always resisted change. I'm not big on it and tend to regard most changes with suspicion and a somewhat mournful attitude. As I watched Susan perform that night, I realized I wanted my little girls back. I missed their honesty, their simplicity, and their interaction. I wanted them to be dancing again in my family room, instead of on a football field like Susan or a stage like Clara. I wanted them to swim in the neighborhood pool together; instead Emma was swimming in an Olympic size pool with girls I didn't know. I wanted them to walk home from school together again, collecting buckeyes and leaves and exchanging confidences. I wanted a piece of their childhood back; just a sliver. I wanted *something* to remain the same.

Susan's squad finished their routine and I mentally shook myself and applauded wildly. I decided to visit the concession stand and as I threaded my way down the bleachers I ran smack into Susan and Clara. Clara was telling Susan what a wonderful job she did and I agreed heartily. Susan looked up at me, her eyes brimming with unshed tears. "Thanks for watching. It's more than some people did! When I ran off the field I saw Emma and asked her how I did and she said she *wasn't even watching.* She missed the entire thing! I'm not talking to her again!"

To give Susan her due, she's not the prima donna that you may think. Yes, she likes to be watched and encouraged. But she also likes to watch and encourage others. For example, she comes to see Clara's plays and is effusive in her praise for them. She likes encouragement because she herself is an encourager.

Emma is not. But Emma is genuine. During halftime, I had noticed Emma leaning on the fence that separated the football field from the bleachers. She had a front row seat for the halftime festivities, including Susan's performance. Truly, she had to work to miss it. Yet miss it she did. And honest she is. If she didn't watch Susan, she wasn't going to soften the blow. She missed the routine. It was simple to her, yet devastating to Susan.

I immediately started soothing. I reminded Susan that Emma was Emma. I told her that Emma loved her despite missing her routine. I mentioned how long they had been friends and told her I was sure Emma was very sorry. From the corner of my eye I saw Emma edging closer. I motioned her in, and she looked at me hopefully. "Did you fix it Mrs. Litavsky?" I heard a great rattling sniff from Susan and decided to take my leave. "I set it up for you Emma," I replied. "Now do your thing."

As I walked away and left the three of them together, I felt a deep sense of contentment. Yes, the girls were starting to drive and look at colleges. Much change had already happened, and much more was to come. But I was comforted.

Not everything had changed. Not by a long shot.

Chapter 9: Learning From Children

"Children are a wonderful gift. They have an extraordinary capacity to see into the heart of things and to expose sham and humbug for what they are."

—Bishop Desmond Tutu

The Sledding Hill

My sinuses were full, my throat sore, and my cough deep. Every bone in my body ached with tiredness; it was a struggle to stay awake during my doctor's appointment. As I drove wearily home it started snowing, and I sighed. This was just what I needed, I thought, feeling extraordinarily sorry for myself. Now, I'd have to tackle shoveling the driveway and clearing mounds of snow off my car for my next expedition. Why, I wondered, was my husband always out of town during large snowfalls? It never failed, just as it never failed that I got sick while he was gone.

The snow was thick and heavy, and fell so steadily that my older children were hoping school would be canceled the next day. To their dismay and my relief, the snow fell short of the foot that was predicted. But as any adult knows, even six inches of snow makes life a bit tougher, especially if you're sick.

It was my turn to drive to school the next morning. After shoveling the driveway, clearing off the car and warming it up, I piled the kids

179

and their mountains of snow gear into the car. As I carefully navigated the slippery side streets, I contemplated a complete location change. Florida sounded pretty good, as did Georgia. That we would have no home or way of supporting ourselves once we got there seemed irrelevant – we'd work out those details with a tan and a smile. We'd save tons of money simply by not having to purchase Land's End coats that needed to be replaced every season. We'd also save a boatload in doctor's bills and prescriptions, as we'd never again be sick. We wouldn't have expensive winter heating bills and we'd never have to spend money to go on spring break. We'd be on one permanently.

I was pulled out of my reverie by my son's enthusiastic voice. He and his friends were in the back seat, examining a foot-long icicle that had somehow found its way into the car with the boys. "Sweet!" he shouted, examining it all over. The boys passed it back and forth. "Mom, this is the best day! Look at the snow! Look at the icicles! This day is going to be great."

I muttered something I hoped would pass for enthusiasm and dropped them off at school. They tumbled out of the car and began to throw snow at each other, screaming with joy. I stuck my head out the car window and narrowly missed being hit by a snowball. "Boys! The bell just rang! Go in now, or you'll be late." They obeyed, walking through as many snow piles as possible before entering the building.

When I got home, I took more medicine and drank cup after cup of hot tea in hopes in helping my head. Nothing was working.

When my son came home from school he announced he needed to go sledding. I assented, adding the back yard was a great place to sled. He stared at me in disbelief. "But Mom! There aren't any hills. What will I sled down?"

I weakly suggested he and his friend could pull each other on the sleds. Wouldn't that be fun? He gave me a level look and decided not to reply.

An hour later I was at the park on the sledding hill. I'd come to the conclusion that being outside certainly couldn't make me feel worse. It could only make things better.

And it did, because sometimes grownups forget simple joys, and sledding is one of them. It's easy and it costs nothing at all. All you need to do is think like a kid. Since we've been kids once ourselves, it's easy to do. We just need to remember we can do it.

My son and his friend screamed joyfully every time they slid down the hill. Sometimes they crashed into the sidewalls and flipped over. Sometimes they had the perfect run, going fast and straight and coasting to a graceful stop. They traded sleds and debated the merits of saucer sleds. They watched with naked admiration as older boys used snowboards. They showed off a bit for a fellow classmate who happened to be a girl. And they laughed and laughed.

I could barely look away from them, but when I did, I was treated to more beauty. I saw three college students cram on a very thin sled, hit a huge bump, and shout with delight as they became airborne. I watched as mothers tried to coax very young children to sit with them on their sleds. I watched a grandfather excitedly place his grandson on a wooden sled. When the little boy appeared hesitant, the grandfather dropped all inhibition. "Scoot forward" he said happily. "I'm going down with you." He arranged himself on the sled, put his arms and legs around his grandson, and pushed off.

Occasionally, I'd walk a bit away from the hill to unleash my dog. The sun was shining on the unblemished snow, making it sparkle like diamonds. My retriever bounded effortlessly through it, leaping high and occasionally stopping to smell. When I called him back, he raced up to me with his face so full of snow I could barely see his doggy grin. His joy quotient was right up there with my sledding boys.

With a start, I realized we had been at the park for two hours. Not once had I thought of my headache or cough. Not once did I wish myself in a different climate. Instead, I had reveled in the simple joy of clear, sparkling snow. When I focused on the positive, I felt physically better than I had in a long time. The afternoon in the snow was better medicine than any I had been taking.

I must remember to view each winter's snow through the eyes of children. They often have much healthier perspectives on things than we do. They see the snow for what it is – a beautiful part of God's creation. They rightly consider it a gift, one that should be opened and enjoyed to the fullest. If the scene on the sledding hill made me smile, I can only imagine what it did for God. After all, He created it.

A Release from the Rules

I t was a beautiful early fall afternoon, and my kids asked if they could ride their bikes. I assented, reminding them to ride only on the sidewalks and to watch out for cars backing out of their driveways. I also mentioned the fact that you could never trust a car's turn signal and despite cars waving you on at a stop sign, you needed to shake your head and motion for the car to go on. I told them that they should only cross a street at a four way stop sign, and only when there were no cars stopped at any sign.

My children assumed expressions of amused forbearance and assured me that yes, they would be very careful and no, they wouldn't forget anything I had just told them. They raced out to the garage, got their bikes and carefully set off on the uneven sidewalks.

I admit to being a bit of a fanatic about street safety. For some reason I cannot understand, I've always been cautious (okay, flat out fearful) about my kids getting injured by a moving vehicle. I know fear is not from the Lord, and I've tried unsuccessfully over the years to banish the fear, but it remains. It's not as strong, but it still pulls on me at times.

My children argue that riding on the sidewalks is just as dangerous as riding on the side of the street, and they in fact have a point. In our older neighborhood hundred-year-old tree root systems have wreaked havoc on the sidewalks. They're uneven, jutting messes. When I go running, I eschew these roller-coaster relics, choosing instead to run on the flat pavement. Call me a hypocrite; I still insist my kids ride on these sidewalks. I feel a collision with a sidewalk or tree can do less harm than a collision with a car, and I still stand by that sentiment.

My kids think I'm a bit over the top about street safety but they usually obey my rules, at least within my sight. There may be some eye rolling behind my back but I never see it.

One day, however, my children got a reprieve from my rules in the form of a block party. As so often happens with children, it wasn't the structured activities that made their day – it was something we really hadn't planned.

The planned activities were simple, yet numerous and kid-oriented. There was a moonwalk for jumping and small pumpkins for decorating. There were piles of streamers and straws for decorating bikes for a bike parade; the decorating was taken very seriously by many kids who worked for hours patiently weaving crepe paper in between their tire spokes. All these activities were big hits, yet there was one unplanned by-product of the party that brought such intense joy to the children it almost brought tears to my eyes.

The street was no longer off limits. The police department had officially blocked off the street, and the entire block was free and clear from traffic. Bikes could be ridden on the street with abandon, pumpkins could be decorated at a table in the middle of the street, and treats could be eaten sitting on a curb.

The kids were off their bikes only long enough to decorate them, otherwise, they were flying up and down the street, jumping sidewalk curbs and screeching to a halt to make tread marks on the streets with their tires. They rode with no hands. They raced each other. But everything they did, they did in the middle of the street.

My son flew by me on his bike, his face a mixture of ecstasy and joyful disbelief. He was literally glowing when I pulled him off his bike to force-feed him a hot dog. "Mom, this is so great," he insisted, shoving his hot dog down his throat and reaching again for his bike. "I'm so glad I'm not riding on those sidewalks! This is a perfect day!"

I had to agree that it was. That sunny afternoon, the street had been changed from something off-limits and potentially dangerous to a hospitable gathering place. It represented a glorious sense of freedom. My daughter and her friends took their piled high plates and ate sitting in the middle of the street. After all, they could.

A few days later we were eating breakfast when my daughter said, very seriously: "Mom, you know the block party we had?" I replied that I did indeed. "It was the best day of my life," she stated rather wistfully. I could tell that she meant it.

Oh, the small freedoms adults take for granted. When we want to cross the street we can. When we want to ride our bikes, we decide where to ride them. Although kids are not limited by their imaginations, they are limited by many rules. They are told when to go to sleep, when to get up, what to eat, and when to cross the street. For my oldest overachieving daughter, a day with fewer rules was "the best day of my life." The block party made breaking the rules legal, if only for a few hours.

Watching my children's joy while they sat in the middle of the street reminded me of our relationship with Christ. Police sawhorses blocked dangerous traffic and allowed them to go places they could never go before. So it is with Christ. He has blocked off sin to allow us to go someplace we couldn't before – heaven. Just as children revel in the freedom given to them by the roadblocks, so we should revel in the freedom given to us by Jesus. He did not give us more rules to follow; in fact He broke the rules to save us.

The Beauty of T-Ball

God provides us with beauty in ways we could never imagine on our own. When we think about beautiful things, we might envision tulip farms in Holland or New England colors in the fall. We don't usually think of baseball fields; in particular, t-ball fields, but places of beauty they are indeed, especially when a real play is made. For example, while watching one of my son's t-ball games, I experienced this shaft of sunlight:

The first baseman caught the ball swiftly and surely, tagged the base, and the runner was called out. The watching parents erupted into cheers and exchanged high fives. The play itself wasn't that spectacular, but it was something. A ball had been thrown, and a ball had been caught. This was cause for celebration. What did we care that it had been our runner who had been called out? In t-ball, any catch is a treat; any play applauded.

Watching a t-ball game is truly some of the best entertainment around. Not only do the kids love it, but the parents aren't uptight about how their kids are playing. The only thing that matters is participation. T-ball is, after all, about learning the game of baseball – the rules, the friendships, and most importantly, the fun. And the things you see during the average t-ball game are, to coin my own phrase, column material.

You see kids sitting down in the outfield or pretending they're Buzz Lightyear swooping about on his hard plastic wings. You notice boys proudly adjusting and readjusting their cups. Yes, boys must wear protective cups for t-ball, even at the tender age of five. When first presented with the equipment list, I laughed out loud, thinking the coaches were joking about the cup, but to my surprise, they weren't. Park district policy. (Finding a cup that small was quite a trick, but the boys seem quite proud; it just adds to their enjoyment of the whole experience.) Many kids throw their mitts up in the air and catch them repeatedly. Occasionally they miss and hit themselves in the face. While the kids in the field are usually looking anywhere but the batting box, the players awaiting their turn at bat are usually pummeling each other. Occasionally, a younger sibling escapes a parent and toddles out on the field.

It's not only the kids who are entertaining. Watching and listening to the coaches is also rewarding. I hesitate to label the coaches as people. They are saints, long-suffering martyrs who give hours of time they don't have to coaching kids who have no idea where first base is. Their patience is legendary.

This is how a t-ball coach readies a player for his turn to bat: "Alright Matt (this is said while fervently clapping), it's your turn to bat. No, turn around. That's third base; home base is over there. O.K. Put on your batting helmet. Good job, but push it down so it stays on your head. Great! Now, get in your stance. No, you're left-handed, remember? Why are you left-handed? We'll talk about that later buddy; just get on the other side of the plate. O.K. Whoa! Don't swing at the ball until I take my hand away from it. O.K. Swing, buddy, swing!"

Anyone who has attended a t-ball game knows this scenario is not an exaggeration. Not only do the coaches give it their all, but many parents also step up during the games and help with coaching the base runners. This may seem generous of the parents — and it is — but it's also completely necessary. Without the first base coach especially, base running would often be at a standstill. The main job of the first base coach is to constantly remind the base runner to watch the batter, so they remember to run to second base. The verbal reminders are punctuated with occasional gentle arm pushes or pats on the head. The batter then needs to be encouraged to run to first base, not stand there and grin proudly when the ball is actually hit off the tee.

All of this effort is worth it. Throughout the hour-long game, I noticed my son glancing down at his uniform with pride. He was so excited to be playing he was literally beaming. He caught my eye and flashed me the thumbs-up sign while a ball rolled gently through his legs. My throat tightened as I reveled in his obvious joy at just being alive: playing ball and tossing his mitt into the air. I think that's what really draws me to t-ball: the unadulterated joy that permeates the event. After all, there's nothing better than an excited and happy five-year-olds, except an entire team of excited and happy five-year-olds. And the icing on the cake is that the joy is realized outside, not in your newly painted living room. So you can enjoy their enthusiasm without a care.

During Rhett's t-ball years, I had no idea whether my son would become a good baseball player, or if his talents would lie elsewhere. And I didn't care. Just watching the games was incredibly satisfying. T-ball contains the best bits of baseball, and its sweetness is fleeting.

I wish there was a way to bottle it for later consumption.

An Answer to Prayer

God can answer prayers instantly.

I truly believe that. I also believe that He usually doesn't. He just doesn't work that way. He's not a genie who grants wishes; He's God. He has his own plan, and His own time.

But sometimes, just sometimes, His plan and time intersects with our own, and our petitions to Him are answered before we're done uttering them. It happened to me a few years ago; I had a prayer answered instantly. Even as it was happening I knew I would write about it. How could I not?

One Sunday my son woke up with the disgusting stomach virus that was sweeping the schools. He was not a pretty sight, and needed to be kept in sight of a bathroom at all times. We immediately adapted and decided to split up for church. My husband went to the early service, the two girls in tow. He got back after 11:00, and I drove directly to a church I used to attend. I knew they had an 11:30 service.

I arrived with only minutes to spare and squeezed in a pew with a dear friend and her husband. Squeeze was the operative word. I knew when their three children were brought in from Sunday school I would have to relocate.

As I relaxed, I glanced around furtively. I was enjoying being with my old congregation again, and wanted to drink in my fill. I looked at babies. Some I knew. Many I didn't. I looked at older couples who had mentored me, and basked in their obvious healthiness. I was glad to see a younger couple who had been struggling with marital problems sitting together holding hands. All seemed well and very well.

There were several families I didn't know, and in my peripheral vision I noticed a wheelchair in the aisle. That person was also someone new to the church, I figured. After all, there was a pastor on the altar I didn't recognize. I'd been gone for a year: a lot changes in a year. I thought idly that it was a good thing this wheelchair-bound person had joined the church recently; the new building that was housing the church was much more handicap accessible than our old sanctuary had been.

When the children filed in mid-service, our pew became too crowded, and I jumped up and headed toward the back of the church. I found an almost empty pew and slid into it.

I was now sitting right behind the wheelchair I had noticed earlier, and was shocked to realize I did indeed know the wheelchair's occupant – and her husband – quite well.

The last time I had seen them she had not been in a wheelchair. She was, however, battling cancer. For a few years it had seemed as though she was winning the fight. This spring she suffered some setbacks, and I had recently heard things were not going well. But nothing could have prepared me for seeing her decline that Sunday.

I was overwhelmed with grief; tears instantly sprang to my eyes and stung my sinuses. Sitting there grappling with my sorrow and surprise, I mentally lectured myself on my comportment. Sorrow and distress were not what this couple needed. They needed prayer, loving touches and words, and support. The service was ending in minutes, and I would be seeing them for the first time in a year. Hysterical tears wouldn't be helpful. I lectured myself; I reasoned with myself; I pinched my arm to attempt to pull myself together. Nothing was working. To my horror, I remained just on the edge of breaking down. That's when I abandoned my own reasoning and simply prayed.

I prayed that I might pull it together enough to give these folks even a sliver of what they needed. I prayed for self-control and calmness in spirit. I prayed that God would give me the right words and gestures for this dear couple.

I lifted my head to see a little girl standing by my side. I had taught Ashley in vacation bible school, and even though I no longer attended her church she still remembered me. She held out her arms and I lifted her onto my lap.

Her cheek pressed against mine as she quietly (church wasn't quite over yet) updated me on her life. Her brother was sick. She was enjoying school. She had gotten candy from her Sunday school teacher. Did I want a piece? Did I like candy? Where were my children? Did they like candy? Did I let them have as much as they wanted? As she spoke, her caramel smelling sweet breath washed over me. Her body felt firm and healthy on my lap. Without realizing it, I became calm once again.

After the service Ashley slipped off my lap and headed toward the coffee hour to collect cookies. I inhaled, felt an amazing serenity, and reached out to my wheelchair bound friend and her husband. I told them how blessed I was to see them again. I listened to updates on their children and gave them updates on mine. I grasped their hands and assured them I would pray. It wasn't much, but it was better than the hysterical tears that had threatened me earlier.

Prayer is indeed powerful, and we're told in scripture it's always heard: *"If you believe, you will receive whatever you ask for in prayer"* (Matthew 21:22). Many times we don't recognize an answer, or ever understand the apparent lack of one. Cancer is an all-too-common example of this. But sometimes, just sometimes, an answer is provided in our time, in a way we can understand.

My prayer for calmness and grace was answered instantly, in the form of a little blond five- year -old girl.

My IT Department

When I purchased my iPhone I felt as if I had made it. I was officially on the cutting edge of technology! My life would become a model of organization: never again would I miss a Girl Scout event or a basketball practice. I would, with help from my iPhone, seamlessly cruise through the scheduling and driving routines that have become my life. It would be my camera, my iPod, my phone, my calendar, my alarm, and my computer. And, when my children are around to help me, it is all these things.

It's embarrassing to have my ten-year-old shake her head sadly at me, take the iPhone from my hand, touch the screen, and hand it back. I should know, I really should know, how to navigate all these scrummy functions on my phone, but I don't. For years, I marveled at how it was that my kids could navigate technology so much easier than I could. Are they smarter than me? (That answer is probably yes but let's not go there right now.) Do they have better reasoning skills? Are they computer nerds, gifted as Steve Jobs? Why can they manipulate my iPhone so adeptly when they are using ordinary flip phones? How do they know what to do?

It finally became clear to me the other day when my son was stabbing at my iPhone screen. I had pleaded with him to help me with a function and as he was tapping away, I asked him how he knew how to do it. He barely stopped tapping as he glanced up at me. "I don't. I'm figuring it out."

This didn't sound good to me. While he was "figuring it out" all sorts of things could happen. My entire address book could be erased. My apps could be deleted. My calendar could be eaten. But none of these things did happen. My son discovered how to access the function I was looking for and handed the phone back to me. Everything was intact.

"Figuring it out" had me stymied. My generation was not encouraged to "figure it out" on our computers. On the contrary, we were sufficiently cowed to the point of never trying to "figure it out." I remember working in publishing in the nineties, hardly the ice age, but long enough ago that technology was an entirely different animal. I had a full manuscript up on the screen when the computer froze. I tapped a few keys experimentally and then called the IT guys on the third floor. They reacted as if there was a nuclear crisis.

"Chris! Can you hear me! Don't touch the keyboard. Don't touch anything or you may destroy the hard drive. We'll be right up!"

Within minutes, Dan the IT guy was at my door, breathing heavily. "Did you touch anything?"

I shamefacedly admitted to pressing a few random keys before I called. Dan took a deep breath, and then exhaled slowly. "Okay, I'll see what I can do. Why don't you take your lunch now? I'll need your office."

I considered pointing out it was only 9:00 in the morning but looked at his expression, grabbed the hard copy of the manuscript and a red pen, and left. I holed up in the conference room and checked in a few hours later. Dan was still at work.

"Almost done. I really don't know what you did. Do *you* know what you did?"

I considered a snide comeback but bit my tongue and meekly admitted I didn't know what I had done to freeze up my computer. Finally I was allowed re-entry but the damage had been done. Almost a full day had been lost and I wound up working past 9:00 that night to catch up.

Is it any wonder why we aren't big on "figuring out" our iPhones and computers? It's how our generation was trained on technology. There were experts, and we were not them. If you weren't an expert, you needed to step away and let the IT department "figure it out." Participation was not encouraged.

Our kids, on the other hand, have been raised on technology that's much more foolproof. A tap on the wrong key won't erase a hard drive or months of work; it just won't execute the function you're seeking. No wonder they're fearless.

Even as I've added this up, I still gasp in distress when I touch something on my screen and realize I've made an error. This involuntary gasp causes my kids to roll their eyes up to heaven. "Mom, chill! Nothing has happened. Let me see your phone." I hand it over;

they touch it a few times, and then hand it back to me. "You need to be calm and patient," they lecture. "If you relax you can figure this out yourself." How the tables have turned!

The upside to this is I really believe our children are learning patience and problem solving. Instead of throwing up their hands and walking away from technological difficulties, as we did, they tap away and accomplish much more than most adults do. After all, they've been allowed/encouraged to work through technological problems since they could toddle. They calmly try and try again to assemble what they want to create – a slideshow, a Power Point presentation for school, or a four-part vocal on Garage Band.

Patience is something I pray for myself almost constantly. I know it's a fruit of the Spirit; therefore, I must have it. It's just not easily seen. In any event, my children's patience comes in handy for a struggling-for-patience woman like me. Instead of calling the IT department on the third floor, I can gasp for help and my resident IT department comes to my rescue.

Like the IT guys before them, they scold me, but unlike them, they love me. They also don't make me take an early lunch.

Chapter 10: Meandering Down Memory Lane

"If any one faculty of our nature may be called more wonderful than the rest, I do think it is memory."
—Jane Austin, Mansfield Park

A Rewarding Shift

Recently I've been feeling overwhelmed – as if I'm fighting to remain upright in the eye of a hurricane. Things are swirling around me at a frantic rate, sometimes so quickly I can barely focus upon them. I'm experiencing a sense of déjà vu, but I've been moving too quickly to contemplate this feeling. Then one evening, as I carried four plates to the dinner table by using my forearm for balance, I remembered.

This was how I felt every Friday evening for three consecutive college summers. They were my waitressing summers, and when I reflect back upon them, I realize they gave me a crash course in life. Even now, over twenty years later, I sometimes dream about weekend shifts at Old Main Inn. They were – literally – crazy.

At 4:45 on a Friday evening, everyone on staff was tense. The atmosphere was that of a football locker room before a championship game. The servers wore determined looks. The management was clapping and assuring us. The busboys were antsy; the cooks poised over their grills. The bartender was reminding us of the drink specials. We were ready to roll.

And roll we did. From 5:00 to 11:00 we never stopped running. If I paused to reflect or ponder I would become hopelessly behind. My only hope was to remain on task.

That's how I often feel these days. I accomplish something, then pivot to the next task. Instead of bringing soups to Table 10, adding the check for Table 12, and requesting extra olives for Table 14, I'm bringing eggs to my son, checking my daughter's homework, and running my other daughter to voice lessons. The players are different, but the game's the same. And the name of the game – in waitressing and in life – is multi-tasking. Waitressing taught me how to multi-task before it became a buzz word; I learned how to pivot on a dime, carry heavy loads and anticipate requests. All these things have come in handy.

Waitressing also taught me the secret of self-preservation. An older, more experienced waitress advised me to smile on hectic Friday nights. She promised that smiling would make me happy even when I felt overwhelmed. And the happier I became, the more I would smile. It was the classic chicken and the egg debate, she insisted. You know what? It still works.

Smiling didn't (and still doesn't) solve everything, of course. It was sometimes hard to smile when customers were furious with you for something that wasn't your fault. Consider this scenario: Another server grabs your prime rib order and delivers it to her table, meaning it's history. You can't exactly yank it away from her customer. (I considered this option on several occasions but thankfully did not act on my impulse.) You rush back to the kitchen to beg another prime rib, pronto, only to be told they are out of prime rib. You have to tell your customer who has waited for 45 minutes he will not be receiving his prime rib. Your tip is non-existent, and a complaint is made to the manager. What to do?

After several weeks, I learned to shrug off these incidents and move forward. I had done the best I could, but things had not gone as planned. Does this sound familiar? Stolen prime rib no longer affects me, but other losses do. For instance, because I was so busy racing around I didn't place my car keys on their regular hook. Now they're gone. Because they're gone, I can't drive to my daughter's classroom event at school. I wind up jogging there and miss most of it. I try to sneak in the back as my daughter spots me, sweaty and panting, and realizes I've missed her program. What to do?

Exactly what I learned to do those Friday nights so many years ago. Shrug it off and move on. If I waste time bemoaning the incident, it won't change anything, but I'll surely miss out on something else.

Those crazy nights also taught me to affirm those who needed it, no matter how frantically busy I was. The main people who needed affirmation during those hectic evenings were my fellow servers, certainly, (you can barely tell you burned your bangs lighting that saganaki, just brush them to the side, you look great), but more importantly, the cooks.

The cooks had it tough. The kitchen was sweltering and they never stopped moving. 10 frantic servers and two impatient managers were demanding things at all times. I know they weren't paid much, and they never got to hear customers compliment the food. That was one of the things I tried to pass along to them. If one of my tables was raving about the ribs, I let the cooks know. They needed – and appreciated – validation. When they received some, orders were produced more quickly; special requests were granted.

This lesson has stuck with me. On nights when I'm overwhelmed and yell at the kids everything falls apart. But when I affirm them, they happily pitch in and cooperate, making the evening a bit smoother. Both adults and children need some affirmation at times. I know I do.

Why did I waitress those college summers? Well, the money of course. I remember limping home and counting my money sitting on my bed. I had shoeboxes of singles that would pay for my college expenses for the upcoming year. Hard as those weekend shifts were, their rewards were great.

I still feel that way. Some nights, as I trudge wearily up to bed, I peek in at my sleeping children and listen to their contented breathing. My heart twists as I study their faces, which still look babyish in the moonlight. As crazy as this shift is, the rewards are great.

We need to remember God gives us only what we can handle. And He also gives us the experience we need to survive in the present. For that gift, I'm especially thankful.

The Baby Blur

O ne of God's greatest gifts to us is selective memory, especially in regard to labor and childbirth. He knows what He's doing, certainly. If the memories didn't disappear or at least blur, the "be fruitful and multiply" admonishment in scripture might lose its allure. However, the actual newborn baby phase is a delight of discovery coupled with the euphoria of new-mother love, and that also seems to have faded away rather quickly, much to my dismay. I never realized how quickly my newborn baby memories would blur until I had a conversation with my sister a few years after my last baby was born.

When my youngest was three my sister found out she was pregnant for the first time. As her pregnancy progressed, questions began flowing at a fast and furious pace, and she began to call me several times a day. It was natural that she reach out to me; in her mind I was an expert. After all, I had three babies in five years; they were still in pre-school and elementary school, hardly college age. Yet, it quickly became clear there were many newborn details I just couldn't remember.

There was, for example, the question about onesies. Since I'm not sure if onesie is a real word, I'll clarify. Onesies are the little cotton undershirts that snap at the crotch over the baby's diaper. When you're pregnant with your first baby, you receive dozens and dozens of these garments. I remember unwrapping hoards of them at my very first baby shower. Some were plain; some boasted cute prints. All seemed impossibly tiny. I smiled and thanked, but I was not quite sure what to do with them. I took them home, washed them in Dreft (that extremely expensive detergent formulated for babies that you only use for your first child) and stacked them up according to color. They took up an entire drawer in the nursery.

My sister also had a full drawer of onesies. She was calling to ask if she needed them all. "Of course you do," I answered, full of parental authority. "You can never have too many onesies. I got a ton of them at my first baby shower."

"Well, what do you use them for?" she asked reasonably. "Do you use them alone, or under clothes? Can you layer them?" I smiled at her innocence and opened my mouth to explain their many uses. Then I closed it. What did I use all those onesies for? Weren't there many that never even got worn? Did I put them under everything, or only clothes that seemed scratchy? Did I just put my baby in a onesie and then swaddle her in a blanket? I truly couldn't remember.

"You can use them any way you want" I hedged. Then, I remembered an actual fact about onesies. "They need to be changed pretty often, because newborn diapers don't seem to contain messes very well. Putting a onesie under a cute outfit may save the outfit from getting stained." There! Genuine advice from a seasoned mother. I was relieved I had remembered something.

My relief was short-lived, however, as my sister lobbed another query at me. "What about all these receiving blankets? Do I need all of these? I've been given 10 of them! What is a receiving blanket, anyway?"

While she paused for breath I made soothing noises and explained. "Well" I said, "receiving blankets are usually used for swaddling a newborn baby. They're cotton, nice and stretchy, and soft." This specific answer, I figured, would be useful to a soon-to-be mother.

"Swaddling? I don't know what that is. How do you swaddle? What does that mean?" I realized, with some alarm, that my sister's voice had raised an octave. I rushed to assure her.

"Never mind about swaddling! The nurses at the hospital will show you how to do that. Besides swaddling, you can use receiving blankets for just about anything. You can use them for . . ." My voice trailed away. What did I use them for after the swaddling stage? My mind raced to remember some concrete uses for a receiving blanket. "You can use them while you nurse!" I crowed triumphantly. "They're perfect for cover-ups while you're feeding the baby in a place that's not quite private."

Silence from the other end of the phone.

"Or," I improvised desperately, "they're great for mopping up spit-ups. They're really very absorbent. Or, you can use them to cover the car seat when the sun gets too bright in the car. They're great for that!"

It sounded like my sister was taking a deep breath in her Colorado living room.

She decided to press on.

"What about all these little tiny washcloths and hooded towels? How many of these will I actually need? Can't I just use a regular washcloth?"

No, I assured her. A regular washcloth is just too big. It will almost cover a newborn baby during his homecoming bath. A tiny washcloth is just what you need when you . . .

"Wait!" my sister interrupted. "You don't give a baby a full bath until his umbilical cord falls off, right? You can't get the cord wet, can you?"

I was saved from answering when my three-year-old fell down and cracked her head on the coffee table. "Heidi, I've got to run! I'll call you back." I hung up and dashed to my daughter's aid. She was thankfully unhurt, just a bit wobbly.

I did call my sister back that day, after I Googled umbilical cord care.

When I think back on my newborn babies, I do remember some things. I remember their smell. I remember how they used to pass out while nursing, with their mouths still pursed and sucking even while they slept. I loved how their hands looked like little stars, and I adored how they fell asleep in their cribs with their little diapered bottoms in the air.

God has allowed me to retain the beautiful memories, while gently blurring the more stressful ones. That wasn't much help to my sister, but it was a blessing to me. He is good indeed.

Vintage Vinyl

I f I didn't know any college students I would never know what's cool. Keep in mind; knowing and being are two different things.

One night Dan, a church friend from Wheaton College, stopped by the house and announced he had just bought a record player.

"You mean a CD player," I prompted him.

No, he insisted. A record player.

"Like for vinyl records?" I asked, disbelieving.

Dan answered affirmatively. He said he was a vinyl fan, and had started collecting music on vinyl LP's. CDs and digital recordings could not touch the sound quality of vinyl, he added.

Well! I thought. If he wants to see a vinyl collection, wait until he sees ours. And I thought they were obsolete! My husband and I might be re-entering coolness with this new craze.

"We've got tons of vinyl LP's," I boasted proudly. "You name it, we've got it. Do you want me to pull out some boxes? You can go through them if you'd like." I started to run downstairs to the basement to locate my treasures.

Dan looked uncomfortable. "Well, the thing is, I'm not interested in your old albums. I'm buying these albums new, and they're usually singles by cutting-edge bands."

I was stunned. Not interested in my Shaun Cassidy and Barry Manilow albums? Scoffing at my husband's prize Elvis record collection? What about Donna Summer Live? That came in a beautiful tri-fold album cover. And why are new bands going back to recording on vinyl anyway? What was going on here?

Music memories started flooding — fast and furious — into my mind. When I was in high school only the rich kids had access to CD players, and then it was because their parents had bought one. Like most new technology they were extremely expensive; the CD's themselves often topped $20. In the early eighties, that was a lot of money. Most of us lived happily with our cassette tapes and big boom boxes.

I'll never forget the first song I ever heard on CD. My friend's father had invested in a CD player, and it sat forbidden in his home office. We waited patiently for an opportunity to try it out, and one day when the father was away, we crept in and grabbed one of the two disks he had purchased. This was common; after you spent the money for the CD player you had very little left for the actual CD's themselves and you often started out with a very modest collection. Not surprisingly, when I look back, both were Who disks. After all, this father was a child of the sixties. We chose Quadrophenia, but weren't sure how to actually listen to it.

After some figuring, we got the CD in and playing. "Love Reign O'er Me" filled the room. The song starts with sounds of thunder and rain, and then goes into a piano solo. I'll never forget it as long as I live.

When the thunder rolled I nearly jumped out of my skin. It surrounded me, wrapping around me like a cloak and shaking the room. My skin tingled. I could almost feel the pelts of rain hitting my skin. When the music itself started incredulous tears stung my eyes. I'd heard the song dozens of times before, but always on a fuzzy cassette tape. This was something else entirely.

After our illegal rendezvous with the CD player, it was no problem for me to abandon my dozens of cassette tapes. It took a while, but CD players and CD's themselves eventually became reasonable enough for even students to purchase. As soon as I could afford a system I purchased one and never gave my cassettes another thought. For a long time I owned exactly one CD, which I still have though I've long since loaded it on iTunes: James Taylor's Greatest Hits.

This transition was not as easy for many children of the seventies, however. My stepbrother Andy (yes, he has the same name as my biological brother you met in Chapter One . . . confusing at times!) is a perfect example. Throughout his teen years and early adulthood he indulged his passion for music by buying vinyl records, and had hundreds to his name. He liked his vinyl albums and insisted they had superior sound quality to CDs. He bucked the CD craze for many years until the recording companies simply stopped producing vinyl and the electronics companies stopped producing turntables. Andy sadly threw in the towel in the early nineties, but has never stopped lamenting his loss. He records his own songs digitally now but has never quite reconciled himself to the demise of vinyl.

I wonder if Andy has heard about the resurgence of vinyl, and what he would say (or scream) if he heard my 18-year-old friend insist upon vinyl because it has superior sound quality to CDs and digital recordings. I'm also wondering if he still has his very expensive sound system from the seventies.

I'll continue to wonder, because I'm not bold enough to break the news about this vinyl resurgence (no matter alternative and small it may be) to him. He's suffered enough music transition and I do not want to be the messenger — bearing in mind the old "shoot the messenger" saying and all of that.

I believe God created us as musical beings. Whether we listen to our iPods or a live orchestra, we yearn to indulge our senses with one of God's greatest gifts to us: music. It's no coincidence, if you think about it, that music is such a vital part of our worship services. Whether it's a praise and worship hymn or a ponderous Wesley traditional piece, music brings us closer to God by breaking down our inhibitions and our self- awareness.

On a practical note, I'll continue to hold on to my Shaun Cassidy albums. Who knows, they may be worth something again one day.

Today's Blessings, Tomorrow's Memories

The restaurant was almost empty when our three families arrived, and for that I was thankful. Most people eating at 8:00 at night do not appreciate nine stimulated children catapulting by their table, even when they are dressed in their best Christmas finery.

There was one diner, however, I was afraid our children might disturb: an older gentleman hunched alone over his salad plate, without even a newspaper to keep him company. I glanced at him, trying to make eye contact so I could check in with him about our noise quotient. He kept his eyes on his plate and continued to eat slowly and steadily. I walked over and laid my hand on his arm. He looked up and met my eyes.

He was much older than I first had assumed; probably every bit of eighty. He wore a cardigan and what appeared to be bedroom slippers with no socks. He did seem serene and alert however, so I figured he was ahead of the game compared to so many seniors I knew.

I asked, in what I hoped was a cheerful tone, if the children would bother him. His eyes seemed to give off a faint twinkle. "No!" he said. "I love children, and I'll enjoy watching them. They'll remind me of old times." I murmured my thanks and returned to our long table, which was right next to his booth.

The next hour was filled with joy for our young families. We had just come from our elementary school Christmas Concert, and all in all, the evening was a success. No one had cried and no one tripped on the bleachers. The songs were sung with gusto and the hand gestures had been made with confidence. Ribbons had stayed in carefully coaxed curls and ties had remained around the skinny necks of our boys. All of us, including the children, had enjoyed the concert. The ice cream we were shoveling in our mouths also added to the sweetness of night.

The adults watched the children interact. We commented on the blessing of their combined good health, and mused on the importance of wonderful neighbors and strong childhood friendships. We laughed when the older girls insisted they needed space from their kindergarten brothers, and we poured water into coffee cups so the littlest girls could have "tea" with their ice cream. We unashamedly basked in our children for that hour.

We reveled in their security, in their happiness, in their very childhood. We felt collectively blessed and fulfilled, surrounded by our neighbors and children.

Occasionally, I glanced at our elderly neighbor. He was very slowly eating his main course, and did not seem at all disturbed by our children. On the contrary, they appeared to provide him with some live dinner entertainment. When the littlest girls authoritatively told their older brothers to sit nicely and wait for their ice cream I noticed a slight smile on his face, and when one of the dads in our group placed his daughter's fluffy bow on his bald head he chuckled along with us.

As the children became weary and slightly shrill we decided to call it a night. I noticed, as we were rising, that the gentleman next to us was attempting to do the same. As I rushed over to assist him, I saw he had dropped some money on the table for a tip and suddenly felt morose that I hadn't paid for his dinner. What had I been thinking?

"Thanks so much," the old man said. "Sometimes, it's pretty hard to get up these days. Oh, and I guess that nice young man at your table bought me dinner. Please tell him thank you. It was so very kind of him."

I was relieved that one of my friends had indeed put his faith into action. What good people I surrounded myself – and my children – with!

As we left I felt absurdly on the edge of tears. It didn't seem right that we had enjoyed such companionship and joy together while an older man sat by himself. I regretted not asking him to join us, but I had felt, frankly, that our group would have been too much for him. Plus, I wanted to leave him his dignity. Why, I agonized, was it so hard to know what to do in these situations?

Later, I sat down to write about the evening, but couldn't think past the salty lump in my throat. I felt we had met that solitary man at the restaurant for a reason. What was it?

I may never know, but I kept wondering if while this man was watching our children, he was remembering. Remembering a time when he and his wife brought their kids out for ice cream after an event. Remembering, as he watched the boys terrorize the girls, how his son used to drive his daughter into tearful furies. Remembering, as he watched our girls drink their "tea", the china tea set he placed under the tree for his four-year-old daughter.

My prayer is that the hubbub of our families resurrected many joyful memories of himself as a younger man, reveling in the health and happiness of his family and friends.

I hope this man reminds me never to wish away time. And I hope I remember that these are precious days, days in my life that I'll never forget. And that someday, I might be sitting alone in a restaurant, watching families gather after a school concert, and remember . . .

Chapter 11: Glimpsing Grace Through Faith

"The grace of the Lord Jesus Christ be with your spirit."
—St. Paul's letter to Philemon

God's Mark

L ately I've been talking to people (men and women alike) who are a bit disquieted. They're feeling they may have missed something – a chance, a risk, a reward. At one time they felt the invincible power of youth; they had everything at their disposal to make a difference. They're now concerned that they may not have made that difference. And they're wondering if their chance is gone.

I've been struggling with the same doubts. When I was younger – in college and the first few years beyond – I was confident I would do something dramatically important. What, I wasn't sure. But something big, something that mattered. My friends felt the same way; I wasn't alone in my excitement. Our newly educated hearts raced with anticipation about the unknown. We were poised on a blank slate. All we had to do was make our mark.

Perhaps because I'm pondering those post college days, I'm re-reading Ayn Rand's The Fountainhead. In it the young hero, Howard

Roark, wants to make his mark on the world (literally, because he's an architect) without compromising his ideals. He knew he had the power of creation, and he gave that power free rein, unafraid of where it would take him. He needed only a blank sheet of drafting paper and a pencil to make his mark. The character of Howard Roark illustrates how many of us viewed our twenties. We were staring at a blank sheet ready for our mark. Anything was possible; we just needed to draw with bold, sweeping strokes. Best of all, we had years to find our purpose. Time was our friend; we had plenty of it.

Yet somehow the time flew by. Seven years after embarking on my post-college journey I quit my job as an editor at a publishing house to have my first baby. I remember seeing no alternative to that decision, yet mourning it. You see, I felt I hadn't made The Mark yet. I hadn't signed that gifted author who would change lives; I hadn't really changed anything at all. Oh, plenty of marks were placed on my sheet during my twenties, but not The Mark. Not The Mark that could somehow change the world.

Three children and many years later, I continue to ponder the fate of my Mark. I'm not alone; most of my contemporaries are in the same boat. We're catching our breath after the small baby years and reassessing our lives. I'm hearing parents ask questions like these: Am I fulfilling my purpose here? Is there something incredible I'm supposed to be doing? Is the purpose of my existence really car pools?

Am I looking only at my family and not the larger world? Is what I do important or self-serving?

Just as there was so much unknown to us in our twenties, so it is today. There are no answers that will please each and every one of us. But I've been focusing on a few thoughts that I find very comforting.

First, God has a plan for each one of us, and if the plan is God's, it's perfect. It may not match our perception of what we should be doing, but we are not in charge. God is, and He's much smarter than us. It is never through our own efforts that we change the world for the better; we can do nothing without God's help.

Second, even if we open up our hearts and minds to being used for God's plan, I believe many of us won't ever see our Mark while we're living. It doesn't mean we won't make one. Perhaps many of us already have. Perhaps we have many more to make. But <u>how</u> God is using us may not be clear to us. For example, I believe that my son Rhett may be part of my Mark. Bearing and raising him may be God's plan for me, because Rhett may be someone who is used by God to advance His kingdom. I felt the Holy Spirit put that on my heart hours after he was born. I don't know what it means or what it will look like, but that doesn't mean it's any less real. I just may not see it while I'm here.

(Sometimes, I must admit, as I tell Rhett for the third time to move his basketball shoes off the counter and the fourth time to write his name on his homework I wonder if I was still reeling from the epidural during my hospital revelation and misunderstood what the Spirit was telling me, but there it is.)

Perhaps most importantly, I've grown in my faith over the years to believe – really believe – that love is the most powerful thing in the world. The more we love, the more we can achieve. We may be making our Mark simply by loving more and more. When I quit my publishing career to take care of my baby I thought I had missed the chance to make my Mark. But it was only through having my baby that I grew in love of God as well as others. If we grow in our ability to love, we're never missing any incredible chance or responsibility. Love is our responsibility.

Armed with these thoughts, we may be more content to sit back and see where God is taking us.

After all, we really have no choice.

God's Favorite Number

Numbers can be deceptively powerful — they can actually take prisoners. I'm proof. Until recently, a number was holding me captive. This number had nothing to do with my finances or my child's grade point average, yet it had everything to do with perceived success. The bible study I help lead has significantly fewer heads this year. Once bursting-at-the-seams, it's slimmed down by half, and that was causing me great anxiety.

I'm not alone in my fixation with numbers. In today's more-is-better America, we're usually seeking loftier numbers. We want numerous bedrooms in our homes, several cars in our garages, and higher balances in our bank accounts. We're a numbers oriented society; trained to seek and expect high numbers, and equate them with success.

But what kind of success? Worldly, certainly. But what does the bible say about the success of large numbers? God does not seem to play the more is better game. The story of Noah indicates that God would rather have true belief than large numbers. Out of all the people who lived during Noah's time, only eight were saved from the flood due to their righteousness. It was from these few that God built his kingdom. In fact, time after time scripture tells us of faithful remnants of God's people who made an impact for His kingdom despite their low numbers.

Naomi's family in Moab is an example. They were indeed small in number, yet they made such an impact on Ruth that she converted to Judaism and contributed to the lineage of Jesus. The disciples are another case in point. Jesus chose twelve, not twelve thousand, and those twelve impacted the world.

And, let's not forget God started with only two people in the Garden of Eden, Adam and Eve. True, He instructed them to be fruitful and multiply, but if numbers were His main concern, He probably would have started with more people from the words "Let there be . . . ."

There is a number that God insists on being very high – and that's the number of people who choose Jesus as their way, their truth and their life. In fact, He is patiently waiting for that number to keep climbing. We should, as Christians, also be focusing on that number, not merely higher numbers in general.

I've realized my bible study is a modern day example of God's faithful remnant. In the past, this non-denominational neighborhood study topped out at 70 women. This year, it's down to about 35 regulars. This is not a slight reduction.

My first reaction, as I've already confessed, was a debilitating fear. Instead of focusing on Christ, I focused on my own abilities. I was determined to identify the problem and fix it. For weeks I spun my wheels trying to increase attendance. Did we need more teachers? Better coffee? Should we include worship songs? More prayer time?

Free babysitting? Finally, I did what I should have done at the outset. I knelt down to God.

As I committed the bible study and its future to prayer, I felt God speak to my heart in a way I don't often experience. I envy my brothers and sisters in Christ who seem to have a clear, open dialogue with the Lord; for me, His voice often seems muffled. But sometimes, just sometimes, God knocks me from my chair with his clarity. This was one of those times.

God told me, quite clearly, to remember my old church, which I loved and was grieved to leave. He reminded me that when everything there imploded, attendance was at a record high. It was the place where everyone wanted to go. But during a theological crisis, it simply fell apart. Higher numbers do not necessarily indicate more people have true belief.

I realized it is the same with the bible study. It is pared down and streamlined, but stronger than ever. The women who attend each week are committed and eager to delve into the Word. The enthusiasm has been infectious; each woman feels accountability and responsibility to the more intimate group. True belief is stronger than in previous years, despite the lower number.

We need to remember the numbers God is interested in are not our sales numbers, or our stock portfolio, or the number of people in our bible studies or churches. What God cares about is the number of people who truly know Him through belief in Jesus Christ.

I believe this lesson is the most important thing I've learned from my bible study yet. God has used decreased attendance to regain my attention, helping me focus on Him, not numbers, for answers and guidance. He has done this for one reason: He loves me.

Since I am only one, this is yet another sign to me about numbers. They don't matter. Our relationship with Christ does.

The Bridge

After several years of searching, we finally found a vacation property. It fit all the criteria I've already written about: it was a delightful eight acre mixture of woods and field. It was private, with the cabin set atop an impossibly steep hill. And it was located off a gravel road used only for local traffic. But the pièce de résistance was the steel bridge that was now our very own. The long driveway that entered the property used to be a county road and the bridge that crossed over the steep banks of the creek was a county bridge. When the land was rezoned the road and bridge became private property, and an enterprising gentleman built a modest cabin that could be accessed only by crossing the creek using the bridge. The bridge boasted the date 1893 on its end cap and greatly added to the character of the place, which we christened Shiloh.

Shiloh quickly became a wonderful retreat for us. As it was only two hours away from our house, we went on weekends as often as we could. It was wonderful to relax, pick raspberries, and take long walks. But the main event at Shiloh was the creek.

The creek was year-round, yet quite benign. Our kids could wade in almost every part of it and the water rarely came over their knees. It was bursting with critters: fish, crayfish, frogs and tadpoles, water snakes, and even a muskrat. We spent many happy hours capturing things, examining them, and releasing them back into the water.

Fishing off our bridge was also a highlight. We only used worms and never caught anything big, but the action was constant enough that the kids never got bored. Life at Shiloh was good.

Yet, worries about the bridge niggled at the back of my mind. I know scripture tells us not to worry about tomorrow, and I was trying, really trying, to simply enjoy our vacation retreat. Yet the bridge kept fussing me. There seemed to be no reason for my concern. We drove over it — as did guests and repairmen – time and again without incident. It was old, but seemed to be in fine shape. Looking back, I think I was worried about the responsibility of a bridge, an actual bridge. Who owns a steel bridge large enough for SUV's and small trucks to safely use? Who knows how to maintain a bridge like that? Or repair it?

It turns out my worries about maintaining and repairing the bridge were academic. We never had to do either.

Two years ago we decided to spend a July weekend at Shiloh, and had the truck packed and ready to go. Before we could depart it started to rain with monsoon-like intensity. We pulled back into our driveway and decided to wait until the morning to leave. After all, it's not much fun to huddle in a tiny cabin in the pouring rain. Shiloh is really an outdoor place.

The rain became even more ferocious during the night and my husband and I jumped up almost simultaneously to check the basement. Although it never had gotten water, there were several inches down there already. We sprang into action and worked for several hours salvaging what we could. Just as we were finishing up the phone rang. We looked at each other. It was not even 7:00 in the morning. This could not be good.

Tentatively I picked up the phone. "Chris," the voice drawled, "this is Dan Johnson calling." My heart sank. Dan's farm was two miles down the road from Shiloh; he had our contact information. "Are you planning to come out here this weekend?" I murmured that we were. "I'd think twice about that if I were you. I don't think you can quite access your place."

I asked if the roads were washed out. "Oh, the roads are washed out all right, but that's not gonna be the problem. You see, your bridge is gone."

I inquired, with mounting dread, if he thought it could be repaired. Perhaps we should come out right away and look at it.

"No," he said comfortably, and I began to suspect he was enjoying himself, "it's gone. Completely washed away. Not a speck is left. The whole darn thing just floated down the crick into Ted Molsen's cow pasture. It's pretty mangled though. Really no way to salvage it."

I hung up the phone and slumped against the wall. My worst fears about the bridge had been realized. It was gone. And we had no way to access our cabin.

I called Ted Molsen, who confirmed that the remains of our bridge were indeed gracing his cow pasture. I offered to call the local salvage place but he interrupted me. "I've got more than I can handle repairing fences from this flood. My cows are everywhere. I can't worry about the bridge and I don't need salvage people messing with my pasture. Forget it! I'll cut it up when I get around to it if I can keep the metal for scrap."

It sounded like a pretty good deal to me, plus Ted was clearly at the end of his rope. I could hear cows bawling in the background, so I hastily said goodbye. A few hours later, when I had gotten over the worst of my shock, I called Ted back with a request that I knew would irritate him and I doubted he would grant, but I had to try. I wanted that 1893 end cap; it was my favorite part of the old bridge. I left Ted a voice message asking him to cut it off the bridge and save it for me. I was not hopeful.

During the next year we met more neighbors than ever before. The loss of the bridge caused many folks to stop by, gaze at the gaping hole between the banks, and reminisce about how they used to fish off our bridge as boys. At times there would be several older men clumped together, chewing on straws and speculating happily about how our bridge would be impossible to replace.

I wish I could write that we've replaced the bridge and all is rosy, but that is not the case. We've noodled through culverts, reclaimed steel bridges and flatbeds anchored with concrete. All these options cost almost as much as the land is worth. We've studied aerial maps for different access points, talked with surrounding farmers, and finally hired a construction team to make us a "crick crossing." A crick crossing entails plowing through the high, steep banks of the creek, leveling them out, and pouring a ton of gravel in the creek itself. Then you drive across with your four wheel drive vehicle. If there's a rain, or too much gravel washes away, the creek rises and the crossing is useless.

This past summer, two years after the bridge washed away, we stopped by Ted Molson's farm to buy berries when he said suddenly, "Oh, I have something for you." He led us to an outbuilding which contained more metal and machinery than the eye could see, and extracted a small piece of metal from the bottom of a pile. It was the 1893 end cap to our bridge, flaking green paint and all.

So a very small piece of the bridge remains with us.

It now sits on my mantel at Shiloh, a constant reminder of what Christ is to us. He is the bridge to God, allowing us to cross a chasm too wide for us to ever cross over alone. Without Christ, God is inaccessible. Just as we can't get to our cabin high on a hill without the bridge, we can't get to God in Heaven without Jesus. We can try to access Heaven other ways – giving a lot of money to charity, volunteering, or going to church every Sunday – but just like our crick crossing, they'll fail us. When it becomes rainy and stormy, the crick crossing won't get us to our final destination. Only the true bridge can do that. And that's what Jesus is to us.

He's the only way to get to our final home on the hill.

Finding Grace in Alzheimer's

My dad and I drove to the Alzheimer's Care Center in silence. We'd been there earlier in the day, and the time we'd spent with my 64-year-old stepmother Dianne had not been good. She'd been anxious and unhappy; she didn't seem to recognize me, or, at times, her husband of almost 30 years. She commenced a fretful pacing a few minutes into our visit and would not respond to activities that had stimulated her only the day before. We had arrived in high spirits but after a few hours our dispositions had changed for the worse.

Adding to the depressing atmosphere was the condition of the other patients, two in particular. Millie was tied into her wheelchair to keep her upright, and thumped continually and aggressively on the attached tray. She was hunched over to the point that eye contact was impossible; although we spent hours hearing her pound the tray I had no idea what she looked like. Adele was a tiny woman loaded with accessories who took an immediate liking to my purse. She had an expectant, almost pleading look that never left her face; she appeared to be waiting for someone who never came. She would trot after us on her dainty feet, and when we left the secure unit we could see her little face peering after us through the window.

As my father parked the car for our evening visit with Dianne, he said, "You know, there's just nothing good in this. Nothing."

I agreed. Alzheimer's is a dreadful disease that holds out no hope for recovery. There's no chemotherapy to battle its progression, no surgery to cut it away from the brain. There was nothing redeeming about the situation we were about to re-enter.

There we sat, two Christian believers, letting despair and doubt lead us away from Romans 8:28: "*And we know that in all things God works for the good of those who love him, who have been called according to his purpose.*"

We knew this truth but in our grief and frustration had temporarily forgotten it. God, in his wisdom, decided to remind us that night.

We entered the secure Alzheimer's unit and the first thing that struck me was Millie's face. I could see it. I could see it because Dianne was tenderly kissing her forehead while holding her hand. Millie was beaming. And she was not pounding her tray.

As we gaped at the scene, Adele decided to join the goodwill. She moved into Dianne's radius and got the same treatment. Dianne soothed, stroked cheeks, held hands, and made the same calming chitchat that she used with my children when they were babies. The effect on Millie and Adele was nothing short of miraculous. They seemed happy and serene, and gazed trustingly at Dianne as she helped them to the dinner table.

My dad and I joined them, both reeling over what we had seen, and what we knew God was showing us. Within five minutes of our determination that nothing good could come out of a situation, God had shown us, quite clearly, that we were wrong. Dianne had given two lonely women a sense of worth and identity. She had listened patiently to their garbled accounts while stroking their hands. She had looked into their eyes, really seeing them as God's creations. And she was treating them that way.

As we sat around the table we mentioned to Dianne that we'd be taking her to church in the morning. My dad caught Adele's expectant eye and asked her if she'd like to join us. "Yes I would," was the immediate reply. The nurse, overhearing our conversation, chimed in. "I'm sure she'd love it. The pastor brings her communion every week, but she can't go to services by herself, and she has no one to take her."

(The Alzheimer's unit is locked up tighter than a drum for a reason. One of the biggest fears of Alzheimer's caregivers is literally losing a patient if they wander or decide to simply leave. They honestly forget they're not walking out their own front door.)

We extended the church offer to Millie as well, who wasn't interested.

The next morning we collected Dianne and Adele and walked into the main hospital to the chapel. Adele was not only ready; she was sporting more necklaces than usual. She sat primly beside me and said all the responses without the aid of the prayer book. I glanced at her and noted her expectant look no longer looked out of place in this tiny hospital chapel with the faux stained glass.

God is so faithful, despite our stumblings. Sometimes, we just need to be reminded of the truths we know, and He reminds us in ways we could never invent ourselves.

Alzheimer's disease is not good, and Christians will get it. As we know, Romans 8:28 does not promise that only good things will happen to believers. It does promise that God, in His ultimate goodness and grace, will make good come out of evil and ugly things that happen in this world. Watching Millie raise her head and stop pounding her tray in frustration was good. Watching Dianne give these women a sense of self-worth, even for only moments, was good. Hearing Adele recite the Lord's Prayer was good. These things came from the bad business of losing someone to Alzheimer's.

When we get to our ultimate home, nothing evil or ugly will happen ever again. We know that's true. Rev 21:4 tells us: *"[God] will wipe every tear from their eyes. There will be no more death, or mourning or crying or pain, for the old order of things has passed away."*

Perhaps that's why Adele looks so expectant. She knows what's to come.

235

100% of all royalties from *Glimpsing Grace in Ordinary Days* will be donated to Timothy Project, a Wheaton, IL based ministry focused on sharing the gospel and love of Christ with people of diverse cultures.

Please visit their website at www.timothyproject.info to learn more about this life-changing ministry.

CPSIA information can be obtained at www.ICGtesting.com
Printed in the USA
BVOW02s2053131113

336212BV00010B/330/P